W9-ACD-997

Ancients and Axioms: Secondary Education

in Eighteenth-Century New England

by Robert Middlekauff

AYER COMPANY, PUBLISHERS, INC.
SALEM, NEW HAMPSHIRE 03079

Reprint Edition, 1988
Ayer Company, Publishers, Inc.
382 Main Street
Salem, New Hampshire 03079

Copyright © 1963 by Yale University Press
Reprinted by permission of Yale University Press

American Education:
  Its Men, Ideas, and Institutions - Series II
ISBN for complete set: 0-405-03600-0
See last pages of this volume for titles.

Manufactured in the United States of America

Library of Congress Cataloging in Publication Data

Middlekauff, Robert.
   Ancients and axioms.
   (Yale historical publications. Miscellany 77)
(American education: its men, ideas, and
institutions. Series II)
   1. Education, Secondary--New England--History.
I. Title. II. Series. III. Series: American
education: its men, ideas, and institutions.
Series II.
LA222.M53 1971   373.74   79-165725
ISBN 0-405-03713-9

183538
BELMONT UNIVERSITY LIBRARY

LA
222
, M53
1988

AAZ-8947

Yale Historical Publications
David Horne, Editor
Miscellany 77

Published under the direction of the Department of History

Ancients and Axioms: Secondary Education

in Eighteenth-Century New England

by Robert Middlekauff

New Haven and London, Yale University Press, 1963

Copyright © 1963 by Yale University.
Designed by John O. C. McCrillis,
set in linotype Garamond type,
and printed in the United States of America by
Vail-Ballou Press, Inc., Binghamton, N.Y.
All rights reserved. This book may not be
reproduced, in whole or in part, in any form
(except by reviewers for the public press),
without written permission from the publishers.

Library of Congress catalog card number: 63-7941

Published with assistance from the Frederick
John Kingsbury Memorial Fund

FOR BEVERLY

Preface

BOYS in eighteenth-century New England entered school at an uncommonly early age according to our standards. They complained about it as boys usually do and probably would not have been comforted by the knowledge that they were following a practice long established in New England—and in old England as well. Much, in fact, that they did in school had long been customary; without knowing it they were participants in an English educational tradition.

This tradition in its New England setting is the subject of this book. When I began to read in the sources, I had no such specific concern; I was simply interested in secondary education (a term which New Englanders would not have recognized but which I have taken to mean the education given scholars between elementary and college years). I soon found that liberal education had had a long life in New England. The tradition was modified, of course; and I have discussed the changes in it (especially in Chapters 2–4 and 9–11).

What differences education made in the lives of boys—a more interesting subject even than the tradition—is one I have treated in the final chapter. It is a subject which deserves much greater study, but because I can think of no way of disentangling the results of schooling from other influences, I have discussed it only briefly. What I have done is to suggest how the tendency of several kinds of education strengthened the bent of cultural development in New England. For the most part my ideas on this matter should be read as speculations.

The research for this book was done in the libraries of Yale, Harvard, and Brown Universities, in the Connecticut Historical Society, Connecticut State Library, New Haven Colony

Historical Society, Rhode Island Historical Society, New Hampshire State Library, New Hampshire Historical Society, Massachusetts Historical Society, Boston Public Library, Forbes Library, American Antiquarian Society, Brown University Archives, and Massachusetts Archives. I am grateful for assistance from the staffs of all these institutions and to the Headmaster of the Hopkins Grammar School, the Principal of Hopkins Academy, and to town and court clerks all over New England. In particular I owe much to Howard B. Gotlieb, Librarian of Historical Manuscripts in the Yale University Library, who suggested that I examine several rich collections which were unknown to me.

Although I have written according to my own understanding of the sources, I have benefited much from the criticism of teachers and friends. Sidney Ahlstrom, Hans Frei, Leonard Labaree, and George Pierson all read an early version of this volume (a dissertation awarded the George Washington Egleston Prize at Yale), and made useful suggestions for its improvement. Lawrence W. Towner gave a part of Chapter 5 (which appeared in the *William and Mary Quarterly*) a careful reading, besides lending me microfilm in his possession. But I am most indebted to three others: Martin B. Duberman, for constant encouragement and perceptive criticism; Edmund S. Morgan, whose work will always be the model for my own, for critical and imaginative guidance from the beginning through the end of the writing of this book; and, most of all, my wife, for help of a kind which can be acknowledged but never measured.

R. M.

New Haven, Connecticut
May 1962

Contents

Abbreviations

AAS   American Antiquarian Society
CHS   Connecticut Historical Society
CSL   Connecticut State Library
MHS   Massachusetts Historical Society
RIHS Rhode Island Historical Society
Yale Yale University Library

Introduction: Establishing an Educational Tradition

PRONE as they were to controversy, men in colonial New England rarely argued about the kind of education their society required. Almost everyone agreed that church and community rested upon citizens able to read and write, and upon leaders trained in the learned languages and the liberal arts. Deprived of these minimum skills and enlightened leaders, they believed, society would give way to sin and anarchy.

Puritans brought these convictions to New England and a determination to give them an institutional form. For a society as hard-pressed as theirs was, sustaining anything more than elementary schools would have been an extraordinary achievement. Yet almost before the Puritans had chiseled out a foothold in the wilderness, they were building schools and a college.

Not all Protestants shared their devotion to education. In England, for example, radical sects flushed with enthusiasm rejected the head in favor of the heart. These groups insisted that God's spirit in man and God's word in the Scriptures furnished all the guidance His creatures required. Profane study, they knew, diverted one from the chief end of life, the glorification of the Lord. In any case, in their striving for salvation, men could be sure that God showed himself to ignorant and learned alike; they could be sure that God demanded only that they believe, not that they exhibit learning in the trivium or the sciences; and they could be sure that when they received grace, knowledge and understanding accompanied it.[1]

1. Perry Miller, *The New England Mind: The Seventeenth Century* (Cambridge, Mass., 1954), pp. 74–81.

I

Puritans never claimed that to be saved men needed the knowledge of the arts and sciences. But they insisted that reaching faith is an intellectual as well as a spiritual process. They were convinced that men's understandings acted almost as powerfully as their wills to bring them to God. For before it inclined a man to God, the will consulted the understanding which—persuaded of God's glory—enlightened it.

Nor did Puritans slight the Scriptures in favor of secular studies. Perusing them as intensively as any sect, they agreed that in them God had supplied the ultimate authority on all religious questions, and many questions outside religion as well. But the Scriptures, they argued, had to be comprehended intellectually.[2]

In this task, men could command reason, one of the great gifts of God. Though tarnished by the fall, reason retained some of its original power, enough at least to fathom dimly God's will. For further light men could probe the natural world for its secrets; God intended that they should, confident that their discoveries would reveal His glory.

What horrified Puritans about the sects was their refusal to admit the validity of these rational ways of knowing. In place of reason the sects substituted the faith that every regenerate man could communicate directly with God. To Puritans their certainty was monstrous egotism and the wildest kind of delusion. In the ignorance of those who mistook their own inner promptings for the voice of God, Puritans perceived a threat to the community they were endeavoring to create in New England. Anne Hutchinson was such a threat; education, Puritans hoped, would prepare people to resist the rantings of fanatics of her kind. In particular it could equip ministers and magistrates with the knowledge necessary to guard the churches and the commonwealth.[3]

2. Ibid., pp. 187–90.

3. Ibid., pp. 74–77. Samuel Eliot Morison, *The Founding of Harvard College* (Cambridge, Mass., 1935), p. 250.

What kind of knowledge? Because all knowledge reflected God's glory, Puritans seized upon all kinds, medieval and modern and pagan and Christian. They were especially drawn to classical literature because they believed that the revival of learning had spurred the reform in religion. There were limits to the uses of the classics, of course. Religious questions could not be settled on their authority; and when heathen writings conflicted with scripture, they had to yield. Yet, for all the restrictions placed upon them, their prestige remained enormous.

If the Puritans' study of the classics, the sciences, and the liberal arts was almost inevitable for children of the Renaissance, so also was their haste in founding a college and schools. Not that educated men were lacking in New England—an extraordinary number of English university graduates arrived in the first fifteen years after the settlement of the Bay Colony. The problem was how to maintain this high level of intelligence; and maintain it they must or give over the purpose in coming.

The Puritans had come on a divine enterprise: they would be a city upon a hill for the emulation of Europe. The society they had left behind had not heeded their calls for reformation; they would found a model society free of its corruptions. Always realistic, Puritans recognized that without men of wisdom and strength—educated men—failure was certain. They knew too that Europe would scorn to imitate a society which did not value learning.

The founders of New England came of age in a society committed to traditional education. Though traditional, it was not obsolescent; it was in fact utilitarian. Men trained in the grammar schools and the universities found their knowledge of Latin and Greek highly useful in the service of church and state. And without a classical education careers in the other professions were almost impossible. Education also opened a way for social advancement, a fact which encouraged the sons of merchants and tradesmen to enter schools and universities.

Because they were so obviously useful, schools in England could draw upon a society eager to fill their needs. Before the break with Rome, they had grown up haphazardly from varied origins. Most were connected with cathedrals, but there were some owned or sponsored by chantries, monasteries, collegiate churches, and guilds, and a few by hospitals. None of them escaped the eye of the Medieval Church, which licensed all schoolmasters, sent its bishops regularly into the classroom, and thus saw to it that boys received the true religion along with the learned languages.[4]

The Reformation fattened the endowments of most of these schools and spurred the founding of hundreds of others. Chantry and monastery schools especially benefited as the Chantry Commissioners endowed many lapsed or decaying institutions. Others prospered from private gifts which increased tremendously as Protestants began to realize, especially under Elizabeth, that the reformed religion needed the buttress of educated men. The Queen's government itself spent little money, but merchants and wealthy churchmen were less tight-fisted. Both groups, zealous to prevent a return to the old faith, gave enormous sums to establish new schools and to salvage those sinking under debt.[5]

Though private benefactions were large in the sixteenth century, the great period of giving and of school founding came under the early Stuarts, when in one forty-year period £383,594 was given in ten counties. Of this sum £220,599 15s., nearly 58 per cent, was applied to grammar school foundations. Even the revolution of the 1640's did not diminish this outpouring greatly, for in those years another £130,461 9s. was given for education. Of this sum grammar schools received almost

4. Thomas W. Baldwin, *William Shakspere's Small Latine and Lesse Greek* (2 vols. Urbana, Illinois, 1944), 1, 285–435. Wallace Notestein, *The English People on the Eve of Colonization, 1603–1630* (New York, 1954), p. 116.

5. Notestein, pp. 116–17. W. K. Jordan, *Philanthropy in England, 1480–1660* (London, 1959), p. 282.

£90,000. Parents and town governments proved generous supporters of schools in this period too. Fees and tuition were collected from parents of scholars, while towns were sometimes forced to allocate taxes or to set aside lands if schools were to be kept open.[6]

Though the national government proved reluctant to endow schools out of its own pocket, it did not hesitate to take a hand in their management. Henry VIII, for example, authorized the schools to use only Lily's *Grammar*. Elizabeth issued a similar order in 1559 and following the old custom continued the visitations of bishops into the schools in their dioceses. Schoolmasters soon learned that they must take the oath of supremacy and must regularly repair to the church if they hoped to keep their places. In other ways, too, the church in the service of the state continued its old dominance over the schools; if anything, Protestant control was tighter than Catholic.[7]

The schools themselves at the opening of the seventeenth century were much like their medieval predecessors. Taught by a single master, who if lucky had the assistance of an usher, the average school received children of all ages. Even grammar schools which preferred to receive only Latin scholars sometimes contained "petties," as the small children learning to read and write were called. Towns were especially prone to crowd all age groups into a single school, believing that such an arrangement demonstrated to the rate-payers that they were getting their money's worth.[8]

In the grammar schools boys concentrated on Latin and gave Greek only secondary attention. They memorized the rules of grammar, disputed with one another in formal exercises about its intricacies, translated Latin into English and then turned this product back into Latin, wrote Latin themes, composed verse, and sometimes put on Latin plays and dialogues.

6. Jordan, p. 283. Notestein, p. 117.
7. Notestein, p. 117.
8. Ibid., pp. 125–28.

After seven years of this, they emerged able to read, write, and speak the language and, if their masters had been especially demanding, with a fair knowledge of Greek as well.[9]

Unaware at first that English achievements were unattainable in the new world, the Puritans carefully imitated the old and familiar educational practices. Harvard, modeled on Cambridge, was begun in 1636, and elementary and grammar schools opened even earlier in several Massachusetts towns. Finding money for these ambitious efforts proved difficult, and a period of experimental finance followed. To aid the college the General Court voted £400, gifts were solicited as far away as England, and parents of boys were charged tuition. Somehow the college stayed open, though its financial status remained shaky for years after its beginning.[10]

Schools resorted to the same hopeful search for funds. Boston, for example, collected a private subscription in 1636 for a master hired the year before. Less confident of its citizens' generosity, Charlestown after granting its master £40 for a twelve-month school year decided to rely on the rates for money to pay him. Other towns in these early years depended on tuition collected from parents; a few relied on income from lands donated by private citizens and public authority; and one, Roxbury, turned the whole problem over to a board of "feoffees," who were to act on the school's behalf just like the trustees of any incorporated English school.[11]

The results were disappointing everywhere. Without steady support schools met infrequently; masters did not hesitate to give up poor-paying jobs in the classroom for steady work elsewhere, and children went untutored. These failures convinced Massachusetts leaders that the state would have to take a hand. But what could it do? In 1642 the General Court came

9. Baldwin, I, 134–37.

10. Morison, *Founding*, pp. 292–324.

11. Samuel Eliot Morison, *The Intellectual Life of Colonial New England* (New York, 1956), pp. 64–65.

up with an answer. It approved an act which required parents and masters of indentured servants to teach their children or servants to read and understand "the principles of religion and the capital lawes of the country." [12] Selectmen were to enforce the law through periodic examinations of children and servants. Compliance with the law was another matter; parents found instructing children difficult, and selectmen despaired of visiting scattered families to listen to children stumble through their primers and catechisms. Moreover, the act set a deplorably low standard: children did not even have to learn to write under its terms and no mention was made of the languages.

Five years later its weaknesses were corrected by an astonishing statute in which the state declared its intention to channel a part of the meager resources of the community into education. This act—later the model for Connecticut, Plymouth, and New Hampshire statutes—placed responsibility for maintaining schools on the towns, by enjoining every town of fifty families or more to provide a school where children could learn to read, write, and cipher, and those of at least one hundred families to support a master capable of teaching Latin and Greek. The Act did not repeal the one of 1642; parents could choose between sending their children to town schools or educating them at home. But at least they could now be certain that schools would be available.[13]

Assuming a determinative role in education was a daring move by the state, but passing the burdens of finance and management on to the towns was a masterful one. It conceded the primacy of the local community in Massachusetts and yet insisted that in education as in other matters of concern to the whole colony, the state would establish standards for all. A bold stroke—but not an obvious one. For by appearing to strike a balance between state and local authority, the statute concealed the novelty of the state's entrance into education.

12. Max Farrand, ed., *The Laws and Liberties of Massachusetts* (Cambridge, Mass., 1929), p. 11. I have altered the wording of the statute slightly.

13. Ibid., p. 47.

The wisdom of the Massachusetts arrangement was not lost on the other Puritan colonies. To be sure, they altered the details of the statute, but the principle it established was scrupulously observed. A Connecticut act of 1650, for example, following the Massachusetts model almost word for word, remained in effect until 1690, when a second act was passed which required only New Haven, Hartford, New London, and Fairfield —the county towns—to keep grammar schools. Plymouth's of 1677 demanded more, requiring towns of seventy families to maintain grammar masters. After separating from Massachusetts in 1679, New Hampshire was content with less, indeed with almost nothing until early in the next century, when it fell into line.[14]

Towns in all the colonies, gently prodded by the courts or by anxious citizens, fulfilled the demands of these statutes. And as population increased, as towns multiplied, so did the number of schools. According to Samuel Eliot Morison only ten or eleven were in existence "an appreciable length of time" during the seventeenth century. This estimate is probably low; in any case about twenty-five can be counted as the new century opened.[15]

These schools helped establish an educational tradition. The constituents of the tradition—the community's devotion to literacy and classical learning, active state support and regulation, and a growing institutional structure—largely account for the vigor which enabled it to survive the decline of religion and the commercialization of society which occurred in the

14. J. H. Trumbull and C. J. Hoadly, eds., *Public Records of the Colony of Connecticut, 1636–1776* (15 vols. Hartford, 1850–90), *1, 554–55; 4, 31.* David Pulsifer, ed., *Records of the Colony of New Plymouth* (10 vols. in 12, Boston, 1855–61), *11,* 247. New Hampshire's legislature did pass a law in 1693 requiring every town to maintain a schoolmaster, but he did not have to be a grammar master. See Albert S. Batchellor, ed., *Laws of New Hampshire* (7 vols. Manchester, N.H., 1905–18), *1,* 560–61.

15. Morison, *Intellectual Life,* pp. 99–101, lists schools in Boston, Cambridge, Roxbury, Watertown, Charlestown, Dorchester, Salem, Ipswich, New Haven, and Hartford.

eighteenth century. But in part the tradition persisted because the forces which were changing New England in the eighteenth century were able to freshen it with new institutions and curricula. Private education in particular proved especially responsive to the needs of New England's businesses, the chief force transforming education. Thus, though the old tradition flourished virtually unchallenged until the American Revolution, it did not remain unchanged.

PART I

THE PERSISTENCE OF THE PURITAN TRADITION IN
EDUCATION, 1700–1783

1. School and Community:
The Village Pattern

EARLY every weekday morning, and usually on Saturdays too, the scholar in the small eighteenth-century New England town took his place in the local grammar school. Just beginning his grammar education, he was about seven years old. He had learned to read and write a couple of years earlier in a dame school, which sometimes served to take a child out of his mother's way—and out of trouble—as much as it did as a place of education. In the grammar school he did not at first find his lessons much different from those of dame school days. There, as in the dame school, he read, practiced handwriting, and on Saturdays recited the catechism.

Around him boys, few older than fourteen or fifteen, learned how to do simple arithmetic problems—"vulgar and decimal"—and an occasional one tasted algebra, geometry, and trigonometry. This older group he knew to be the "Latin scholars," boys preparing for college through the study of Latin and Greek. In an ordinary day they spent far more time pondering the vagaries of Latin syntax and grappling with books written in Greek than on mathematics or anything else. These older boys, engaged in classical studies, gave the school its name and standing as a grammar school, though it conformed to the Elizabethan model no more than did its seventeenth-century predecessors.

The Latin scholars, whom the young boy would join in a year or two, may have awed him. The same could not be said of his surroundings, which were not only unimpressive but uncomfortable. The school building was small, about eighteen feet by twenty, with a low ceiling and only one or two windows. Sometimes its windows lacked glass (seen in all times by boys as a target) and often its roof, sievelike, admitted the rain.

Inside, in the winter, the boy heard his fellows ask frequently "Master m' I go to the Fire," for the school's one room was cold and only the lucky few close to the fireplace were warmed by it. In the summer the building's walls did not stop the heat. And in the best of weather the scholar found the oak benches solid but never soft.

Presiding in these simple surroundings was the master. Fresh from Harvard or Yale, he was not hard enough, or foolish enough, to enforce the rigid discipline parents have always praised—and yearned to see practiced on the neighbors' children. But he did keep his charges hard at work and thereby directed boyish energies along manageable lines.

The master, as the boy dimly realized, had a better weapon than the rod; too young to be paternal or even avuncular, he nevertheless ruled with moral authority. For he had been commissioned by the town to implant virtue and morality in his charges as well as learning. He might be seriously defied only by one willing to provoke the displeasure of the surrounding adult world and especially of parents.

For the master this trust implied serious responsibility. Fortunately the way to fulfill his duties was well understood. Every morning he led his charges in prayer; at the end of the day he ordered one of the older scholars to recite the Lord's Prayer in Latin, thus joining piety to instruction—a combination dear to the eighteenth century. Occasionally he commanded the boys to stand and then gravely, and perhaps a little pompously, lectured them on the utility of the Christian virtues. He did not deliver a sermon, nor did he discuss theology; his task at such times was to fill his listeners' heads with thoughts of goodness, not to give them religious instruction, which, everyone agreed, was better left to ministers. The school's purpose remained something else: to give its scholars learning.[1]

1. This section is based on many sources. For the dimensions of schoolhouses see *Muddy River and Brookline Records 1634–1838* (Brookline, Mass., 1875), p. 134;

Though the school was not an adjunct to the church, it held a place almost as important as the church's in the life of the town. In most villages it alone offered instruction in Latin, Greek, and simple mathematics. In many it alone taught small children reading, writing, and arithmetic. Even in villages boasting a writing school or two, the grammar school instructed "readers," "spellers," and "cypherers."

It was a combination writing and grammar school. The Puritans gave it this shape in the seventeenth century, for when they first established schools their rude situation did not permit separate writing and grammar schools. Watertown's first school, founded in 1650, illustrates how formless the Puritan school was, compared to the grammar school in England. At first, besides Latin it taught reading, writing, and bookkeeping to boys, and it accepted girls "that have a desire to learne to write." [2] In the next century Watertown, like other towns, supported a writing school or two, but its grammar school continued to train writing as well as Latin scholars. A few towns tried to preserve the old classical structure. The people of Woburn in 1699 sturdily declared that their school was "not to Instruct Children to Wright," it was "A gramer Scool . . . only a gramer Scoole." But three years later they gave up their attempt at institutional purity and invited back servants who obviously were not going to study the languages. [3]

By adding to the curriculum, the eighteenth-century village grammar school tried to do more than its English predecessor. It did so at the behest of the community, responding to public demands because unlike the English grammar school it rarely possessed institutional independence. Even when it did, as in the case of the Hopkins School of Hadley, it still had difficulty re-

Records of Duxbury, Mass. (Plymouth, 1893), p. 208; *Town Records Dudley, Mass.* (3 vols. Pawtucket, R.I., 1893), *1, 76*. For broken glass and roofs in need of repair see *Watertown Records* (8 vols. Watertown, Mass., 1894–1939), *5*, 202, 220, 235, 250, 303, and passim. For a contemporary description of a grammar school see *The Providence Gazette*, Sept. 29, 1764.

2. *Watertown Records, 1,* 21.

3. The quotation is from Woburn Town Records, May 24, 1699, City Clerk's Office. See also meeting of Mar. 2, 1701/02.

producing the traditional lines. Indeed the blurring of the old form can be observed most clearly in the histories of the independent grammar schools.

These schools—in New Haven, Hadley, Ipswich, and Roxbury—were endowed more richly than most town schools and were managed by corporate bodies of sorts. Their founders intended that they should be grammar schools of the Elizabethan type. Yet all admitted "readers and writers" during most of the colonial period.

Their failure to live up to their founders' hopes grew from a number of conditions common to almost every village in New England. In no town were there more than a few students who, preparing for college, desired training in the languages; and at no time in the colonial period was there only one way to get that instruction. Many ministers in need of extra income readied boys for college; and by about 1750 in the larger villages private masters were willing to teach for a moderate fee. So the grammar schools could not always depend upon sufficient numbers to make their existence as classical schools worth while.

Above all, each school had to contend with the village in which it was located. Nurtured on the sanctity of thrift and having lean resources in any case, the village insisted that the grammar master should teach children reading, writing, and arithmetic as well as the languages and thereby relieve the public purse of the strain of paying a second master. No independent school—not Ipswich, Hadley, New Haven's Hopkins, or the Roxbury Latin—proved entirely able to resist this demand.

Until the General Court of Massachusetts came to its rescue, the Ipswich grammar school was probably the least successful of all in fending off the encroaching town. From the middle of the seventeenth century an independent group of self-perpetuating trustees ran all school affairs and managed the school's endowment, which had been gathered from both public and private donations. Despite the private character of the school's government the town continued to contribute to it—"ten acres of marsh" in 1696 and twenty-five pounds in 1714.[4] Accompanying this last sum were the strings that often go with such gifts: the town received a voice in appointing a master and persuaded the trustees that reading, writing, and arithmetic should be taught in the school. During the next six years committees from the town worked fairly harmoniously with the trustees. But in 1720 after a bitter dispute the town assumed full authority over the school. The trustees remained silent for thirty years, and gradually died off until 1750, when the last of their number appointed a full board.[5]

The new group in a memorial to the General Court soon challenged the town's right to control the school and its endowment. After considering this memorial and the town's reply, the Court created a new body of trustees composed of the old four and of three selectmen from the town. The four old trustees remained self-perpetuating; the selectmen, of course, sat under the town's thumb. The compromise worked well: the bickering stopped, and the two groups handled school affairs smoothly. But the pure classical curriculum remained a thing of the past, as readers, writers, and Latin scholars continued to jostle one another on the school's benches.[6]

Though the Hopkins School in Hadley, Massachusetts, enjoyed more success in resisting town control, it too became a combination writing and grammar school shortly after opening. The school had been endowed by a legacy from the estate of Governor Edward Hopkins in 1664, and in the following eleven years three citizens of Hadley had also given it lands. The town, probably sensing that with this auspicious start the school could be made into a going concern without the support of rates, added to its holding in 1666, 1671, and 1678.[7]

4. "Ipswich Grammar School Documents," in Col. Soc. of Mass., *Transactions*, 35 (Boston, 1951), 293.

5. Ibid., pp. 293–94. Thomas F. Walter, *Ipswich in the Massachusetts Colony* (2 vols. Ipswich, 1917), 2, 277–78.

6. Walter, 2, 279. *Acts and Resolves, Public and Private of the Province of Massachusetts Bay* (21 vols. Boston, 1869–1922), 3, 892–93; 4, 807.

7. For a generally reliable account of the Hadley school see *History of the Hopkins*

At first the town managed the school, but in 1669 at the insistence of William Goodwin, one of the executors of the Hopkins estate, a board of private trustees was appointed. Goodwin chose three whom the Hadley meeting approved, and the town selected two. Goodwin himself was to be a trustee as long as he lived. The agreement between Goodwin and Hadley made the board self-perpetuating with full control over not only the Hopkins bequest but also property already given or to be donated in the future. All other matters, curriculum and the appointment of masters for example, the agreement ignored.

The town, reading in the agreement only a limited authority for the trustees, proceeded to make its weight felt in most areas of the school's government. It hired the master and fixed his salary. It directed parents of boys of at least six years to send them to school and to continue sending them until they reached twelve years or attained "a ripeness and dexterity in Inferior learning as writing and reading." [8] It enforced its order by collecting fines varying from five to eight shillings from those who failed to comply. It also collected tuition from parents of attending boys—in 1680 twenty shillings a year for a Latin scholar and sixteen shillings for one in English. All this it accomplished without consulting the Hopkins trustees.[9]

And the trustees? Since the agreement with the town said nothing about the control of these matters, they did not protest. Besides, they had the endowment firmly in their own hands —or so they thought. For several years their complacency appeared justified. They invested the school's resources in a Hadley corn mill and sat back to watch the annual return pile up. It

---

Fund, Grammar School and Academy, in Hadley, Mass., 1657–1850 (Amherst, Mass., 1890). There is a list of early gifts to the school on pp. 28–31. See also Records of the Town of Hadley, Jan. 14, 1666, Town Clerk's Office.

8. Hadley Town Records, Dec. 21, 1676.

9. For the Hadley-Goodwin Agreement see Hadley Town Records, Mar. 20, 1668–69. For town action in hiring the master and collecting tuition see the meetings of Dec. 21, 1676; Jan. 10, 1677/78; Jan. 22, 1677/78; Oct. 15, 1678; Feb. 7, 1680.

did for a few years, until King Philip's Indians burned the mill in 1677.[10]

The next ten years saw the mill's recovery impeded by a legal tangle involving the trustees and the agent who had operated the mill for them. Deprived of its customary income, the school opened only intermittently. The town, sympathetic for ten long years, finally lost patience in 1686 and resolved to prop up the faltering school in its own way. First it took over the endowment and then, ignoring the trustees, appointed its own committee to manage school finances. But before this group could really get under way, the trustees appealed the seizure in the county court. Here they won in 1687, when the Hampshire County Quarter Sessions ordered the return of the school's estate to them.[11]

Repulsed by the court, the town never again succeeded in grasping financial control, though it clung to the fiction that some power over that part of the school's estate which earlier meetings had contributed still resided with it.[12] Nor could it retain authority over schoolmasters who after 1693 were appointed by the trustees alone. Yet it did get its way on one crucial matter—the school continued to receive scholars on the elementary level. Occasionally citizens conscious of the terms of the Hopkins legacy reproached the trustees for acceding to their violation. But not even Israel Williams, one of the Connecticut Valley's River Gods, who in 1759 urged the trustees to eject the English scholars, could move that body to alter an arrangement sanctified by practice and public opinion. The English scholars stayed throughout the century.[13]

10. *History of the Hopkins Fund*, p. 36.

11. Hadley Town Records, Aug. 22, 1686; Aug. 29, 1687; Feb. 6, 1687/88.

12. See, for example, Hadley Town Records, Mar. 25, 1751; Mar. 5, 1753.

13. A glimpse of the school committee's techniques of management can be seen in the School Committee Book, a book of rough financial entries, Hopkins Academy Principal's Office. Israel Williams' attempts to restore the school's classical emphasis can be reconstructed in the following letters: Israel Williams to the School Committee, Jan. 1, 1759; Israel Williams to ? [1759]; Samuel Cooke to Samuel Hopkins, July

If the independent grammar school had little success in preserving traditional institutional form, it at least escaped many
consequences which the public grammar school—owned and
operated by the town—could not. In its periodic meetings the
town handled the school in just about the same manner that it
did any public business. This was a fact of enormous importance: the school could not avoid the impact of ordinary town
politics and of public financial pressures. New Englanders would
not have had any other arrangement. They knew what they
wanted in education and believed that no better means of getting it existed than that provided by the town meeting.

As Americans have been ever since, New Englanders were
beguiled by investigations of public problems, by reports, and
especially by committees. Hence, it is not surprising that for
the actual administration of the policy formulated in meeting,
the town looked to a special committee or to the selectmen acting as one.

In its choice of men to direct the school, the town demonstrated its belief that schools, though they should take their
place in the political arena like any other public concern, deserved the best talent available. For the men charged with administration of the schools usually had more political experience
than most citizens. If a town had wealthy and educated men,
they too usually served at one time or another. (Ministers, of
course, never had a hand in town government, and, therefore
no part in running public schools.) In 1700, for example, Hartford appointed a committee filled with leading townsmen. Four
years later it chose a new committee, dropping two men from
the old and adding three others; in all, seven different men
served on the two committees which managed the local grammar school for the first dozen years or so of the century.[14]

1766; Letters and Papers Relating to Hopkins Academy, Forbes Library, Northampton, Mass.; Israel Williams to ?, Apr. 5, 1766, Israel Williams Papers, MHS.

14. Hartford Town Votes 1635–1716, in Conn. Hist. Soc., *Collections*, 6 (Hartford, 1897), 258, 277, 305.

All owned land, several, substantial amounts. Two, Aaron Cooke and Captain Cyprian Nichols, were men of modest means, leaving estates valued at about £250. The others were wealthy: Joseph Talcot left an estate valued at almost £11,000; Richard Lord had over £6,000 when he died; John Haynes over £3,000; and Thomas Bunce over £1,000. The group was as rich in political experience as in money. Besides serving as an assistant from 1708 until his death in 1713, John Haynes also sat on the bench with his fellow committeeman, Judge William Whiting. Haynes and the others participated in town government, too. Five were selectmen at one time or another, and several held lesser offices. Only Haynes, son of an early Massachusetts governor, had a college education.[15]

Watertown, Massachusetts, provides another example. Until 1766 Watertown had left its schools to the selectmen. In that year, perhaps because the selectmen's duties were growing burdensome, the town resorted to a committee elected annually in the town meeting. From 1766 to 1776, twenty-five men served at various times on a committee which usually numbered five. Two men served a total of six years each and a number of others two and three years; fourteen served only one year. Three of the twenty-five were Harvard graduates—an unusually high proportion, indicating that Watertown believed in using its educated.[16]

Most of these men seem to have been farmers. At least one was a craftsman who made coffins, tables, and chests; another probably was a tavern keeper, for periodically he was licensed as a retailer "of Spiritous Liquors"; one had kept the grammar school forty years before, turned to land speculation, and then,

15. For their land holdings I have used Hartford Town Votes, Conn. Hist. Soc., *Collections*, 14 (Hartford, 1912). For their estates see Charles W. Manwaring, *A Digest of the Early Connecticut Probate Records: Hartford District* (3 vols. Hartford, 1904–06). For their political experience see Hartford Town Votes, passim.

16. *Watertown Records*, 5, 310, 328, 343; 6, 2, 18, 38, 54, 80, 94, 132, 141. The graduates of Harvard were Nathaniel Harrington (A.B. 1728), Samuel Fisk (A.B. 1759), and Samuel Barnard (A.B. 1766).

once more answering the town's need, came back to the school-room from 1768 to 1770—this time at a salary much fatter than he had received before.[17]

Like Hartford, Watertown relied upon men experienced po-litically. All had held minor town offices before 1766. David Bemis, for example, had been a constable, deer reeve, fence viewer, surveyor of highways, warden, and clerk of the market. In 1766 he took his place on the committee which annually examined the treasurer's accounts. None of these posts ap-proached the selectman's in importance, but they did give a man knowledge of the town's problems and experience in deal-ing with its citizens—useful skills for the work of school super-vision. Six had also been selectmen many years, and at least one of the six sat on the committee every year except two.[18]

Committee functions varied little from town to town. Al-most always when a committee was used, it hired the school-master, found a place for the school to meet if a regular building was lacking, and handled the finances of the school. In most towns the committee was allowed to hire a master in its own way, though it did have to satisfy the meeting. In Massachu-setts a statute added another requirement: the local minister with one of his brethren, or any two neighboring ministers to-gether, were supposed to approve the grammar school master before he was hired. Though evidence is lacking, towns seem to have observed this statute. Only rarely did cases concerning noncompliance get into the county courts.[19]

17. Ibid., 5, 84, 203; 6, 26, 46—for the craftsman (David Bemis) and the tavern keeper (Jonah Copen). Nathaniel Harrington was the old master brought out of re-tirement.

18. For Bemis' political experience see *Watertown Records*, 5, 210, 236, 251, 265, 279, 309. To sample the experience of the others see ibid. under their names: Jonathan Brown, 5, 292, 309, 325, 342; 6, 1, 16, 35; Moses Stone, 5, 342; 6, 1, 16, 35; Deacon Samuel Fisk, 5, 16, 18, 86, 119, 136, 157, 168, and so on.

19. The Mass. statute is in *Acts and Resolves*. Job Palmer's certificate declaring him fit to teach, signed by two ministers of Middleborough and one of Plimpton, is in the Penniman MSS Coll. filed with his MSS Navigation Book, Yale. A similar certificate is printed in *Records of the Town of Plymouth* (3 vols. Plymouth, 1889–1903), 2, 229–30. For further evidence that the law was observed see Records of the Court of

Hiring a master did not usually prove difficult. Harvard and Yale replenished the supply every year with young men who turned to teaching while they prepared for the professions or looked for opportunities in business. Men in this half-way station between college and career came cheaply—a fact which made them especially attractive to school committees. A graduate's character and academic record were supposed to be much more important in recommending him to a town than his selling price, but towns sometimes overlooked them in favor of a bargain. Watertown, a village not perceptibly slower than most to punish breaches of the Seventh Commandment, snapped up Benjamin Shattuck in January 1708 hardly a month after his expulsion from Harvard for fornication. His pay: "fifteen pounds for the half year," at a time when near-by towns gave their schoolmasters three to five pounds more. Shattuck remained at Watertown for six years at the same salary. His successor, more pure (or more discreet) while at Harvard, was so free from fault that he won the intellectual patronage of Cotton Mather. And at Watertown he managed to collect six pounds a year more than Shattuck had.[20]

If Watertown displayed shrewdness in hiring the ardent Shattuck, other towns sometimes showed a tightfistedness that denied them any master at all. A genuine problem lay behind this excessive frugality: education was often the greatest single expense a town had to bear before the Revolution. This had been so when settlement first took hold and when great wealth did not exist in New England. Only a generation after schools were built, they, along with homes and businesses, suffered the devastation of King Philip's War. Schools recovered from the In-

General Sessions of the Peace . . . for Essex County, Dec. 27, 1715; Mar. 17, 1718/19; Jan. 29, 1723/24; and Records of the . . . General Sessions . . . Hampshire County, 2, 19 (May 20, 1729).

20. *Watertown Records*, 2, 185, 190, 191, 194, 197, 201, 204, 205, 207, 208, 213, 216, 217, 223, 224. For a different version of the town's motives see Clifford K. Shipton, *Biographical Sketches of Those Who Attended Harvard College*, 5 (Boston, 1937), 492–94. Shattuck's successor was Robert Ward. For Mather's praise of him see Shipton, 6, 350–52.

dian war; wealth increased tremendously by 1700—and continued to increase. Nevertheless, paying for education remained a heavy burden. Plymouth, Massachusetts, for example, spent twenty pounds for schools in 1700, almost one-third of its total public charges of sixty-five pounds. Nearly the same ratio continued until the Revolution—in 1769, a representative year, it paid slightly more than seventy-two pounds out of total charges of £230. Plymouth's expenditures for education were higher than most; still, the average town allotted at least one-fifth of its total annual appropriation to educating its youth.[21]

Just as local rates on polls and estates supplied most ordinary town expenses, so did they school expenses. Many towns had another source of income: lands donated by the province, by individuals, or set aside by the towns themselves. Rented, leased, or sold, they furnished a capital stock which towns frequently appropriated for the use of schools. Shrewdly invested, such income could often relieve the ratepayers of a significant portion of heavy school charges. Watertown evidently made such an investment in 1735 with the proceeds from the sale of certain common lands. By 1745 this capital reserved for the school's use "for Ever" returned enough interest to pay the grammar master's entire salary of £100 (old tenor).[22]

If like Watertown many towns had lands set aside for schools, few seem to have been able to make them pay well enough to meet all school expenses; the chief source of income for schools had to be the ratepayer's pocket. Only in Connecticut could towns look to the provincial government for consistent financial help. Connecticut towns received an annual contribution out of provincial taxes of forty shillings on every thousand pounds of rateable estate within their limits. But few, if any,

21. *Records of the Town of Plymouth*, 1, 276; 3, 215.

22. *Watertown Records*, 3, 121; 5, 2. Old tenor was a Massachusetts currency which depreciated badly. In 1750, when the province returned to "lawful money," 1 shilling sterling was by law equal to 10s. old tenor, or 1s. 4d. lawful Massachusetts money. See *Acts and Resolves*, 3, 430–31; and Andrew F. Davis, Currency and Banking in the Province of Massachusetts Bay (New York, 1900), passim.

found the "country money," as the provincial subsidy was called, large enough to meet the expenses of their schools.[23]

For Coventry, Connecticut, for example, a village of less than 1,600 people, the country money totaled £32 13s. 9d. from 1729 to 1732—almost £11 a year. School expenses for these years including £84 5s. 3d. paid to school dames and masters, and £40 10s. 10d. spent for a new schoolhouse came to £125 16s. 1d. Conventry had to find £93 2s. 4d. to add to the colony's funds. This it did by leasing its school lands for 999 years and lending out the income from them at what must have been rather stiff interest rates. On a principal of £357, earned presumably by the lands at rent, it collected a fat £107 2s. in the three years. This amount allowed the town to meet school expenses with £13 19s. 8d. left over, a sum it thriftily lent out again.[24]

One other source of finance for schools existed—the parents of boys who attended. They could be assessed tuition for every child they sent to school and in the early eighteenth century occasionally were. In some towns parents paid tuition directly to the master, as in Watertown in 1700: six pence a week for each Latin scholar, four pence for a "writer," and three for a "reader." In other towns the town treasurer received the money; in Braintree the rate was five shillings per year for children of residents and twenty shillings for those of nonresidents. Though few collected tuition, almost every town required parents to provide firewood in the winter, usually from one-half to one cord per child. Parents also purchased pens and paper for their children, and schoolbooks, since towns furnished only a Bible for the master.[25]

By about 1730 wood, paper, and pens represented the sum

23. For the laws providing provincial support of education see Trumbull and Hoadly, *Public Records of the Colony of Connecticut*, 4, 331; 5, 353.

24. The figures on which my computations are based are in Coventry Town Meetings 1713–1782, Committee Report, Feb. 7, 1731/32, CSL.

25. *Watertown Records*, 2, 132. *Records of the Town of Braintree* (Randolph, Mass., 1893), p. 51. See also New London Town Meeting Records, Feb. 13, 1748/49, City Clerk's Office; Plainfield, [Conn.] Town Meeting Records, Jan. 28, 1708/09, CSL.

of parental contributions in all but a few towns. As they came
to recognize that charges on parents could meet only a small
part of educational expenses, towns relied less on tuition for the
rest of the century. Concurrently, the awareness grew that public taxation offered the only means of meeting the statutory requirements which placed responsibility for education with local
communities. Towns, of course, continued to draw on private
sources for school finance whenever they could, but rarely with
the expectation that such sources would render taxes unneces-
sary.[26]

Whatever source or sources a town relied upon for school
support, it had somehow to offset the erosion of money value
that inflation and depreciation of currencies constantly brought.
This was especially true in Massachusetts, particularly for those
schools dependent upon income from land leased for long periods at fixed rents, until Thomas Hutchinson stabilized the currency with Louisbourg gold in 1751. A school relying on such
income—like Roxbury Latin, which gave some 500 year leases
—could hope to make income equal expenses only when it could
renegotiate leases at higher rents. In the case of Roxbury Latin
even the gains made at such times were soon lost to new inflation and continued depreciation of currencies.[27]

Since most schools were supported by taxes rather than fixed
rents, they enjoyed some immunity from inflationary and currency problems. Town appropriations for schools could be increased frequently even if fixed rents could not—and as a
matter of fact were raised frequently in most villages in the

26. Among Massachusetts towns which stopped collecting tuition early in the century
were Braintree, Watertown, Hadley, Plymouth, Salem, and Woburn. In Connecticut,
New London and Hartford may have required payment of tuition for a time in the
seventeenth century; neither charged parents shortly after the opening of the eighteenth
century. Fairfield seems never to have collected tuition.

27. For a brief account of Thomas Hutchinson's stabilization policy see Malcolm
Freiberg, "Thomas Hutchinson and the Province Currency," New England Quarterly,
30 (1957), 190–208. For Roxbury Latin and inflation see Richard Hale, History of the
Roxbury Latin School (Cambridge, 1946), pp. 54–69.

eighteenth century. This proved to be the only effective method of meeting inflation.[28]

In any case, schoolmasters suffered more heavily from inflation than the schools did. Occasionally a town, taking pity on its master, pegged his salary to the cost of living or the value of silver. Josiah Pierce of Hadley agreed in 1742/43 to a salary of £115 a year in "Bills of Public Credit Equal in Value to Bills of the Old Tenor" or in "Lawful Silver Money at the Rate of Twenty Eight Shillings pr Ounce." [29] In case the bills of credit depreciated below the ratio of thirty shillings to one ounce of "Good Coined Silver," his employers, the school's trustees, were to make good his salary at that rate. On the other hand, if the bills of public credit increased in value above twenty-six shillings to an ounce of coined silver, his salary was to be discounted. As his salary increased until stabilization in 1751, the agreement seems to have worked well for Pierce. Unlike most others, Pierce had an additional cushion in the twenty-five acres of school lands which he was allowed to use.[30]

During the worst period of inflation, schools found young Harvard and Yale graduates as eager as ever to occupy the masters' great chairs. Since the quality of masters remained high, no falling off in the standards of learning seems to have occurred.[31]

Town growth intensified financial problems and created fresh difficulties. As its once compact population increased and spread out, a village saw its single grammar school become inadequate.

28. See, for example, Watertown's school appropriations in 1704, £15 for a half year; by 1715 it was £18 for a half year; in 1717 it was £40 for one year; in 1722, £44 per year; in 1727, £45; 1733, £55; by 1745, £90 per year. *Watertown Records*, passim.

29. "Agreement between Josiah Pierce and School Committee," Feb. 28, 1742/43, MSS in Forbes Library.

30. Ibid. See also Shipton, *Biographical Sketches*, passim, for similar treatment of ministers.

31. Some of Harvard's brightest lights taught during the period of inflation. See

Far from the original settlement, children could not attend the one-time centrally located school. Nothing, of course, prevented a town from providing a second more accessible grammar school. —nothing except money. To soften the clamor for education that arose from outlying districts, many towns decided to up-root the school and send it out on the road. The school might "go round with the Sun," as it did in Duxbury for many years, meeting successively in the four quarters of the town for three months at a time.[32] Putting the school on the move had the obvious disadvantage of spreading learning very thin. A boy who had attended the school for nine or ten months out of a year when it was located in one place might only be able to attend the moving school the three or four months that it was near his house. If he was determined, he might follow the school as it traveled from one spot to the next. But this was so diffi-cult and expensive a process that probably few boys did it.[33]

If many towns sent their grammar schools into remote dis-tricts, many more kept them fixed near the center of town and installed writing masters in the outskirts. This at least assured a minimum education to all quarters of the town. Plymouth, Massachusetts, tried this arrangement for a number of years in the early eighteenth century and steadfastly refused to support more than one grammar school. But in 1722, to ease the thirst of its scattered population for Latin and Greek it turned the grammar school into a moving school, which first met for six months near the center of town, moved for three months to Eale River, and then moved again for the final three months of the year to Manoment Ponds at the other end of town.[34]

This arrangement lasted a year. It seems to have been ended at the instigation of citizens from the populous center of town

Clifford K. Shipton, "Secondary Education in the Puritan Colonies," *New England Quarterly*, 7 (1934), 646–61.

32. *Duxbury Records*, p. 320.

33. A town usually prohibited children from other communities from attending its school; districts may also have followed this practice.

34. *Records of the Town of Plymouth*, 2, 217–18.

who wanted a grammar school fixed to one spot accessible at all times to their children. During most of this period citizens at the extreme ends of town did win a share of public revenue— either outright subsidies or their shares of the rates—for the support of reading and writing schools. The center did not tender this subvention gracefully. Plymouth meetings in the 1720s and 1730s heard "long debates" on the matter—several like the one of February 1724/25 which adjourned in "great tumult" seem to have had abrupt endings. The upshot of the dispute was that in Plymouth, as in most towns, the grammar school stayed at the center and the outlying districts had to be satisfied with elementary schools.[35]

On the move or fixed at the center of town, the grammar school remained as much the community's product in 1783 as it had been in 1700. Towns exerted even greater power in education at the end of the colonial period than at its beginning, because time and experience had perfected the devices of school management. Firmly ensconced in town meetings, the committee system yielded fairly steady and continuous supervision; and finance, though still relying in part on private sources, gradually had been recognized as a community responsibility.

Yet, though the town gave the school its very existence and dominated it in so many ways, the grammar school proved less subservient to the community than to an ideal. From the beginnings of New England the ideal of a liberal education through the study of the classics had been associated with the grammar school. And though almost every town insisted that its grammar school must serve a broad constituency by teaching elementary subjects as well as Latin and Greek, few challenged the ideal. Indeed, far from questioning classical education, towns which never hesitated to make their wishes felt concerning the smallest detail of finance rarely instructed masters how to teach the languages or what textbooks to use. Hartford once ordered its school committee to instruct the master "with Regard to the

35. Ibid., 2, 220, 230, 232, 238–39, 280–83.

Rules he shall observe, the Method of teaching, and of admitting
of Schollars . . ." and Northampton twice warned masters that
they "spend no more Time with the Latin Scholars than their
Equal proportion with other Scholars," but evidence of this type
of supervision appears infrequently in town and committee
records.[36] Traditional liberal education, of course, represented
learning which few could claim to possess; and the majority of
New Englanders probably cared little about the substance of
classical education itself. But they did respect the intellectual
excellence which the classics upheld, and they admired the power
of a liberal education to further a man's career. Even the poor-
est country parson could testify that a college degree raised a
man's status. And all knew that the path of the professions lay
through a liberal education.

Still, New England held a surprisingly narrow conception of
the ends of public-supported education. Just as the classical curriculum remained unexamined, so also did the possibility that
education financed by the community might serve other aims—
as, for example, vocational training. Boys in search of such
training knew that the grammar school had little to offer them
and looked elsewhere. And all the while in town meetings their
fathers confidently continued to tax themselves to support
schools teaching Latin and Greek. This singlemindedness and
this sublime lack of interest in fresh possibilities for public-
supported education bespoke, perhaps as plainly as anything
else, the extent of the village's commitment to traditional education.

36. Hartford Town Votes (1717–1796), p. 204 (pagination in pencil), City
Clerk's office. J. R. Trumbull, *History of Northampton* (2 vols. Northampton, 1902),
2, 304, 358.

2. Variations in the Village Pattern

THOUGH the overriding similarity of the culture of the villages created a pattern in public secondary education, there were variations from one colony to the next. These resulted from local conditions, especially from the amount and character of the provincial government's entrance into the problems of education. No colonial government supervised education through a central agency, or took more than occasional notice of local educational activities; but Massachusetts, Connecticut, and New Hampshire established colony-wide standards which they expected local authorities to enforce. Only Rhode Island's Assembly ignored education completely.[1]

In Massachusetts the statute which required every town of at least one hundred families to maintain a grammar school placed enforcement of the law with the General Sessions of the Peace. With its broad authority and commanding powers the Quarter Sessions (as the General Sessions of the Peace was called because it sat quarterly within the county) was not to be tampered with lightly. Its jurisdiction included all criminal cases except those requiring the death penalty or disfigurement, and cases on appeal from justices of the peace. Coupled to its judicial powers was extensive administrative authority. The court in fact governed the county, laid taxes, and spent them mostly for public buildings, bridges, and highways. It supervised and checked many town functions including "warning-outs" and town bylaws. It issued licenses to innholders and, after 1750, to persons who sold excised goods—tea, coffee, snuff, and china ware. Thus formidably equipped, the court entered village life

1. See Introduction.

whenever it saw the need. Even selectmen were awed by it.[2]

Enforcement of the school laws called for great discretion in the judges. They had to recognize that the disposition of New Englanders to provide education was not always capable of overcoming a stronger propensity to limit public spending. Furthermore, they had to concede that education laid a heavy burden on the public purse—and that towns of one hundred families sometimes had good reasons for not meeting their obligations under the statute. Finally, they had always to keep in mind that education was the end the law looked to; heavy fines or other judicial action which inhibited town support of schools defeated its purpose.

King Philip's War delivered the first great blow to education in Massachusetts. Philip and his allies destroyed eight towns and forced settlers to abandon others; and many more towns received heavy damage. Settlement in the Connecticut Valley retreated twenty miles to the south; fur trading and farming suffered; families were split or deprived of heads. Heavy as its losses were, the colony would have recovered them fairly easily had the forty-year period following given it peace. Instead, settlements in the Connecticut Valley and the eastern ring of towns on the edge of the wilderness from Amesbury to Mendon trembled under a succession of attacks by French-led Indians. Haverhill, Groton, Lancaster, Chelmsford, Sudbury, Brookfield, Marlborough, Billerica, and others were hit—several many times.[3]

Schools did not flourish in this unfriendly atmosphere. Parents hesitated to send their children through woods filled with savages; towns hoarded their meager resources for garrison

2. This estimate of the exercise of the power of the courts is based on my own reading of the Records of the Court of General Sessions of the Peace of Hampshire, Berkshire, Middlesex, Worcester, and Essex Counties. (They are located in the Clerks of the Court's Offices in the various counties.)

3. Douglas E. Leach, *Flintlock and Tomahawk: New England in King Philip's War* (New York, 1958), pp. 243–44. Thomas Hutchinson, *The History of the Colony and Province of Massachusetts-Bay* (3 vols. Cambridge, 1936), *1*, 343; *2*, 62, 67, 75, 78, 80, 82, 110, 121–22, 128–29, 134, 141, 150–51.

houses and soldiers; and young Harvard graduates—who did most of the teaching—preferred peaceful places like Cambridge to the frontier. The neglect of education did not go unremarked: the ministers began complaining of the "Languishing state" of the schools, and the General Court began investigating the state of learning in the colony.[4]

Frontier towns remained demoralized until peace was finally made in 1713. Yet educational standards did not collapse, and few communities were allowed to let their schools close for more than several months at a time. Many wanted to, but their wishes encountered the implacable resistance of the Massachusetts Council and the county courts. The Council took a simple but firm stand: it would listen to pleas for the suspension of the school laws but it would not suspend them. It turned down Chelmsford, a town which had been struck repeatedly by Indians, and which petitioned in 1710 for exemption from the law for the remainder of the war on the following grounds:

> . . . our habitations are very scattering & distant one from another, so that altho' a school were placed in the Centre it would be very remote from the greater part of our Inhabitants, & our Children in passing too & from the same would be so greatly exposed to the snares of our Lurking Enemy, that very few would Venture to send them to school in such danger.[5]

The lower house of the General Court usually acceded to such appeals and to several which would have relieved all frontier towns of educational responsibility, but it never convinced the Council that a change was necessary.[6]

In fact the Council's insistence that there must be no slackening in educational effort carried the General Court to a tighter educational policy. In 1701, complaining that the statute of 1692 (which reaffirmed town responsibility for education) "is

---

4. Massachusetts Archives, *58*, 213–16, 237–38, 276–77.

5. Ibid., pp. 276–77.

6. Ibid., p. 240.

shamefully neglected," it raised the fine on a town delinquent in maintaining a grammar school from ten to twenty pounds.[7] Seventeen years later it stiffened the penalty once more; thirty pounds was to be collected from a town of 150 families which failed to comply, and forty pounds from one of 200 families. Many towns, the legislators commented at this time, preferred paying a fine to supporting a master. The new statutes attempted to reverse things by making the penalty higher than a master's salary.[8]

The General Court cashiered the delinquent towns too confidently. For in court before the Justices of the Quarter Sessions many towns managed to exhibit compelling reasons for their failure to provide schools. In Middlesex County, for example, the court heard twenty-nine cases involving ten towns which had failed to supply grammar masters for varying periods in the years between 1700 and 1720.[9] In only four cases did it judge the towns' conduct so reprehensible that it fined them.[10] Two towns convinced the court that the war prevented them from keeping a Latin school open. Though it agreed that war posed difficulties for grammar schools, the court ordered these towns, Marlborough in 1705 and Billerica in 1709, to keep reading and writing schools in their place. Marlborough and Billerica in the words of the court in 1709 were "out Towns . . . Exposed . . . to Danger by reason of the Enemy." [11] Location along the frontier did not in itself provide an excuse; a town had to produce evidence that keeping a grammar school constituted a hardship before the court would release it from its obligation.[12]

7. *Acts and Resolves*, 1, 470.

8. Ibid., 2, 100.

9. The towns were Reading, Sudbury, Woburn, Lancaster, Framingham, Billerica, Chelmsford, Concord, Malden, Marlborough. Records of the Court of General Sessions of the Peace of Middlesex County, Clerk of the Court's Office, volume for years 1692–1723. (Hereafter this volume will be numbered 1.)

10. Sudbury was fined twice, see ibid., 1, 122–23, 265; Chelmsford once, 1, 128; and Marlborough once, 1, 124.

11. Ibid., 1, 236.

12. See, for example, the case of Chelmsford, ibid., 1, 238–39.

War proved less troublesome to four towns than the scarcity of masters. These were years of small classes at the colleges, and young graduates enjoyed a sellers' market. Chelmsford's experience was typical. In its search it applied to President Leverett of Harvard, but neither he nor others consulted could provide a master. Though the Chelmsford school remained vacant for several months, the court collected no fine; nor did it in the cases of the other three towns. But it did order all of them to maintain writing schools while they carried out their search.[13]

The court was just as understanding and just as firm with Malden in 1710 when that unfortunate town showed that many of its 100 inhabitants were so needy that it could not afford to pay a grammar master. Malden, the court decided, should not be compelled to furnish a grammar master but in his place it must provide one capable of teaching reading and writing.[14] In the remaining sixteen cases all the towns either had grammar masters at the time of their appearance in court—though most of them do not seem to have had them at the time the grand jury brought its indictments—or so speedily obtained them that the court saw no need to collect fines.[15]

In contrast to this early period, only eighteen presentments for default in keeping grammar schools in Middlesex appear in the Court Records from 1721 to 1764—six in the 1720s, two in the 1730s, three in the 1740s, four in the 1750s, two in the 1760s, none in the 1770s, and one in 1780.[16] In only four cases did the court collect fines.[17] The falling off in presentments and

13. The towns were Reading, ibid., *1*, 180; Billerica, *1*, 293; Chelmsford, *1*, 301; Lancaster, *1*, 317.

14. Ibid., *1*, 253.

15. Ibid., *1*, passim.

16. Ibid., *1*; and volumes for years: 1723–1735 (hereafter numbered 2); 1735–1748 (3); 1748–1761 (4); 1761–1771 (5); 1771–1790 (6). The towns and the years they were presented: Chelmsford (1721, 1724, 1742), *1*, 394, *2*, 29, *3*, 289; Billerica (1721, 1724, 1727), *1*, 401, *2*, 25, 126, 424; Weston (1737), *3*, 64; Stoneham (1737), *3*, 89; Littleton (1748), *4*, 3, 33; Groton (1748, 1780), *4*, 20, *6*, 234; Westford (1750), *4*, 133–34; Framingham (1750), *4*, 133; Hopkinston (1757), *4*, 441; Stow (1758), *4*, 492; Sherburn (1761), *4*, 62; Newton (1762), *5*, 79.

17. Chelmsford (1742); Framingham (1750); Sherburn (1761); Newton (1762).

the restrained use of the fine did not mark a slackening of
enforcement. Rather, the problem of enforcement had eased as
wealth increased and towns found the financial burdens of education easier to bear.

Nevertheless, the Middlesex Grand Jury remained vigilant,
perhaps even a little too eager on the law's behalf—as Westford
had reason to believe in 1750. Near the end of May of that
year Westford's population reached one hundred householders—
a number which of course obligated it to set up a grammar
school. In August the grand jury discovered that no grammar
master had been hired, and in December it brought Westford
before the bar. In court the town admitted the truth of the
charge but insisted that it did not have one hundred householders who paid taxes. This, it claimed, exempted it from the
grammar school requirement; and after talking it over, the
Justices agreed and dismissed the case.[18]

The Justices in Worcester County operated differently—at
least for the first thirty years after the county was established
in 1731. Theirs was a subtle compulsion, with fines always
threatened but never imposed. The procedure followed an almost ceremonial pattern: a town presented by the grand jury
appointed agents who appeared in court, relayed their town's
excuses, and accepted the justices' unvarying verdict of guilty.
This completed, the same agents just as regularly proceeded to
persuade them that the fine should be abated or that judgment
should at least be postponed. Usually the court did not allow
itself to be convinced that action should be suspended without
first extracting a promise that the town would provide a school.
In the next term—following the initial presentment—the town's
agents once more appeared to notify the court that their town
now employed a grammar master and produced the minister's
certificate attesting to it. The entire action would cover only a
few months—Uxbridge, presented August 19, 1746, persuaded
the court to continue its case until November 14, when agents
appeared, testified that the town had a grammar school, and

18. Middlesex Records, 4, 133–34.

heard the charge dismissed. The only expense to Uxbridge was the court costs, probably at most two pounds.[19]

This leniency did not always work in favor of education. From 1731 to 1765, the year the Worcester Court first collected fines, eighteen towns failed to provide grammar schools, while ʾn the same period only nine towns were delinquent in Middlesex County.[20] Furthermore, in Worcester there was an egregious tendency among several towns periodically to allow their schools to lapse. The Uxbridge and Brookfield schools closed on three occasions, and those in Lunenberg, Harvard, and Sutton twice. The grand jury seems also to have been affected by the court's attitude. Once it failed to act for five years while the town of Harvard disregarded the statute. And when a presentment was brought the court postponed judgment, after finding Harvard guilty according to form. Harvard then hired a master, informed the court at the next session, and had the satisfaction of seeing the case dismissed on the payment of costs.[21]

In the West, Hampshire County granted delinquent towns less forgiveness than either Middlesex or Worcester. Between the opening of the century and 1783 Hampshire's justices heard thirteen cases in which towns clearly had failed to maintain grammar schools for various periods of time. Eight guilty towns paid fines.[22] The history of the other western county, Berkshire, demonstrates that though the wilderness could blunt the drive for education in Massachusetts, it could not stop it altogether, and that, as elsewhere, the Quarter Sessions took a leading part in enforcing educational standards.

Few white men lived in the territory that was to become

19. Records of the Court of General Sessions of the Peace of Worcester County, 2, 172.

20. The Worcester towns, several more than once: Lunenberg, Harvard, Brookfield, Uxbridge, Lancaster, Sutton, Shrewsbury, Sturbridge, Mendon, Worcester, Woodstock, Leicester, Westborough.

21. Worcester Records, passim; for Harvard, 2, 339–40, 344.

22. For the Hampshire towns that were fined see the Records of the Court of General Sessions of the Peace of Hampshire County, 10, 129 (Amherst, 1770); 10, 176 (South Brimfield, 1771); 4, 23 (Springfield, 1741); 5, 256 (Brimfield, twice in 1756); 5, 260 (Northfield, 1756); 5, 134 (Sheffield, 1752); 6, 168–69 (Brimfield, 1766).

Berkshire County until after the British victory at Quebec in 1759. Before that time anyone settling there invited attack by French-led Indians. This unappealing fate kept all but the brave or the foolish out; and in 1761, when the General Court created it, Berkshire could count only 700 families scattered among three towns and four plantations.[23] During the next fifteen years they were joined by so many others that by 1776 population had increased to almost 18,000.[24] Except for people from New York and Rhode Island, these new inhabitants were of old Puritan stock from Massachusetts and Connecticut. Their origins are important—they brought with them an old cultural tradition. Connecticut's demands upon her towns had not been as high as Massachusetts', but the tradition of public-supported schools was long established.

For leaders, both lay and religious, Berkshire County relied upon Connecticut men; in talent and background they were an impressive group—almost all the early clergy, for example, were graduates of Yale College. These men presided over a society more interested in economic growth than in educational strength, and they were only partially successful in persuading Berkshire citizens to found and support schools. As elsewhere, the General Sessions of the Peace came to the aid of education, demanding that Berkshire towns—despite their youth and poverty—meet the requirements of the educational statutes. The Court had no cause to take action about grammar schools for the first few years after the county's founding, for as late as 1765 only Sheffield had as many as one hundred families—and Sheffield had maintained a grammar school since 1750.[25] But in the next eleven years, fourteen other towns increased in popu-

23. Richard D. Birdsall, *Berkshire County, A Cultural History* (New Haven, 1959), p. 19.

24. E. B. Greene and V. D. Harrington, *American Population before the Federal Census of 1790* (New York, 1932), p. 39. The population figures given in the next paragraph are from this book.

25. Josiah Gilbert Holland, *History of Western Massachusetts* (2 vols. Springfield, 1855), 2, 583. Sheffield was fined in 1752—see above.

lation to one hundred families. Not all showed the requisite speed in founding schools, and the grand jury began issuing presentments. Of the five towns appearing in court before 1776, four were found guilty and fined.[26] The fifth escaped with a warning. As in Middlesex sixty years earlier, not even the vigilance of the Court produced a perfect performance. Evidence is sparse but it shows that most—perhaps all—of these towns supported schools. Some were grammar schools, several probably were not.

In all counties the courts attempted to operate so as to encourage the towns to keep their schools open. The courts were seldom unreasonable or harsh; they recognized the purpose of the law and attempted in every way to see it achieved. Heavy fines, the justices seem to have believed, would be self-defeating, for public money was scarce in every community. Thus fines were calculated scrupulously according to the law—if the fine for a year's delinquency was twenty pounds, six months amounted to ten pounds, not a shilling more or less. The courts always accepted a town's plea that it had been guilty for only a part of the time charged. Richmond in Berkshire County was charged with failure to supply a master from November 30, 1771, until late August 1772, a period of almost nine months. The town's agents admitted that their town had no school for five months of the time, but as for the remaining four they pleaded not guilty. The court did not press the matter and collected £8 6s. 8d. for the five months.[27] The justices used fines as a club, threatening to bludgeon offending towns, and doing so when the law was clearly violated.

Reluctant to fine and almost always willing to postpone, to suspend judgment, to listen patiently to all kinds of excuses, the

26. For the Berkshire towns see Records of the Court of General Sessions of the Peace of Berkshire County, Vol. A, 100–01 (Great Barrington, 1772); A, 110–11 (New Marlborough, 1772); A, 113–14 (Richmond, 1772); A, 111 (Sandesfield, 1772).

27. Ibid., A, 113–14.

courts for the most part provided sympathetic yet careful administration of the law. And except in Worcester County, they
kept the towns up to the mark. This usually proved easy
enough, for most towns consistently observed the law and therefore never appeared in court. The result was that as villages
increased to one hundred families grammar schools sprouted all
over Massachusetts. In the seventeenth century about nine
towns outside Boston were able to maintain grammar schools for
an appreciable length of time; in the eighteenth century this
number grew until in 1765 at least sixty-five towns supported
schools.[28]

Just how important the school law and its enforcement were
can be seen by comparing Massachusetts to Connecticut, where
no comparable law existed in the eighteenth century. Throughout most of the seventeenth century Connecticut had a "one-
hundred family law" modeled on the Massachusetts statute of
1647, but in 1700 it discarded it in favor of another which
required only New Haven, New London, Hartford, and Fairfield—the four county towns—to maintain schools. To enforce
the law, the colony relied on a provision that prohibited the
payment of the country money to any town failing to comply
for more than one month.[29]

For three of these towns, maintaining a grammar school
proved a great trial. The fourth, New Haven, agreed in 1668
to an arrangement proposed by John Davenport according to
which an independent and self-perpetuating board of trustees
managed the school. Eleven years before, Davenport had been
named one of the executors of the estate of Governor Edward
Hopkins, who on his death left about £400 for the support of
a grammar school in New Haven. Between 1660 and 1668, following a suggestion by Davenport, the executors and the town

28. The eighteenth century figure is tentative—based on Court Records, Town
Records, and local histories.

29. For Connecticut's educational acts see Trumbull and Hoadly, *Public Records of
the Colony of Connecticut*, 1, 554–55; 4, 31, 99; 5, 353.

together administered the bequest for the school. Joint control worked badly; disagreements between Davenport's group and the town became so absorbing that the grammar school was seldom open. Davenport, who had never relinquished title to the estate, tired of the fight in 1668 and declared the agreement null and void. No more money would be turned over to the town, he warned, until it yielded full control of the school to a private group. Naturally reluctant to lose anything that would lessen the town rates, New Haven's voters agreed. But suspicious old Davenport did not grant a free hand even to the trustees, and retained a veto on their actions as long as he lived. His other requirements were reasonable enough: the trustees were to manage the endowment, maintain a school building, and hire a master learned in Greek, Latin, and Hebrew. The trustees did his bidding, and though the Hopkins fund—supplemented in 1672 by a gift of 600 acres of land from the colony and by further private donations—was sometimes mismanaged, the Hopkins Grammar School taught New Haven boys throughout the period.[30]

About one hundred years later, Fairfield too gave up its grammar school—not just to a committee but entirely. During the first half of the eighteenth century, the town never quite managed to keep one open regularly. The problem in Fairfield was simple: the town could not raise enough money for a school. Presumably Fairfield received the colony's contribution to education, but this was evidently not enough. In 1752 the town appealed to the General Assembly for help, declaring its desire for the "benefit and Advantage of such a School." [31] The Assembly considered a scheme which would have allowed the town to use a part of the receipts from an excise on liquor levied

30. For the early history of the Hopkins school I have used the Records of the Hopkins Grammar School in the possession of the school. See also Thomas B. Davis, Jr., *Chronicles of the Hopkins Grammar School, 1660–1935* (New Haven, 1938), pp. 83–151. The agreement of 1668 is printed in F. B. Dexter, *New Haven Town Records, 1649–1684* (2 vols. New Haven, 1917–19), 2, 230–35.

31. Connecticut State Archives, College and Schools, First Series, 1657–1762, 1, 131a, CSL.

within Fairfield County, but in the end both houses turned the plan down.[32] Fairfield waited three years more and then in 1755 divided its school lands among the local parishes.[33]

Hartford had much better fortune. Like New Haven it received a little over £400 from the estate of the late Governor Hopkins and 600 acres from the colony in 1672.[34] As in New Haven, generous citizens added to this endowment from time to time with gifts of land.[35] The town itself made gifts—in 1736, the rent from a ferry across the Connecticut River.[36]

If careful management had accompanied this generosity, the grammar school would have flourished. Davenport had not attempted to take the school in Hartford out of the hands of the people, but for a time around the middle of the century some must have wished that he had. Under the supervision of a special committee appointed by the town, the various holdings had fallen into such a tangle that no one knew exactly what property belonged to the school. The school opened only irregularly, and the town could not pay its expenses.[37]

The town first awoke in 1749 when it discovered that the school's endowment did not return enough income even to pay current expenses. Mildly disturbed, it instructed the school committee to lease some school lands on the east side of the Connecticut River which had hitherto lain untapped. The committee seems to have followed instructions, but no great increase of revenue flowed in—probably because the committee continued to give the endowment only indifferent care. In 1765 the town took notice of the "declining State of the Grammar School"— declining to the point of not opening at all—and deciding to do something about it,[38] appointed a new committee with instruc-

32. Ibid., 1, 131b, 132.

33. Fairfield Town Records, Vol. B. pt. 1–2 (Town Meetings, 1681–1826), meetings of Mar. 31, 1755 and Oct. 25, 1787 (no pagination), CSL.

34. Hartford Town Votes, 1, 144. Public Records of the Colony of Connecticut, 2, 176.

35. William D. Love, The Colonial History of Hartford (Hartford, 1914), p. 272.

36. Hartford Town Votes, 1717–1796, p. 95.

37. Ibid., p. 204.

38. Ibid.

tions designed to put the school's holdings on a profitable foot-
ing. To find out just what property the school owned, the
committee was to inventory its holdings. If the committee found
that its securities could not be renewed every two years, it was
to sell them. Besides this, the committee was to call in loans with
interest outstanding, and all loans under fifty pounds. It was
also to introduce a system of bookkeeping—an instruction
which by itself suggests why the school's purse had always been
empty.[39]

These orders governed the financial side of the school for the
rest of the century. The committee, to which additional members were appointed from time to time, was left largely on its
own, though in 1782 the town casually approved its conduct
under the regulations established in 1767.[40] Apparently this
confidence was merited, for the committee thereafter managed
the school's endowment with vigor and care. In 1776 it obtained
the Assembly's permission to sell five hundred acres of the
colony grant of 1672, which had remained unclaimed up to that
time.[41] By the 1790s—and probably earlier—it had organized
itself so that one of its members served as a treasurer who saw
to it that debtors of the school settled their interest payments
on time.[42]

Hartford had long vested its school committees with other
duties besides managing the endowment. In the 1760s the town
aimed at higher educational standards as well as financial sol-
vency. So, throughout the remainder of our period the committee worked under instructions to supervise the master and
students by periodic inspections and attendance on the school's
exhibitions.[43]

Unlike Hartford's, New London's grammar school committee
never allowed the school's financial affairs to fall into a muddle.

39. Ibid., pp. 204, 212, 214.
40. Ibid., p. 294.
41. Connecticut Archives, 2, 38.
42. Hartford Grammar School Records, 1790–1947 (no pagination), Trustees
Meeting, Dec. 23, 1793, CHS.
43. Hartford Town Votes, p. 214. For exhibitions see pp. 187–88 below.

The committee itself was not permitted freedom enough to do so. Every year it had to appear before the town meeting with a financial accounting. It was also chosen annually, though usually the same men were appointed year after year.[44]

New London must have been pleased by the size of the school's endowment. In 1749 its holdings amounted to at least £603 and probably more. These capital assets were carefully hoarded, perhaps too much so. For example, in 1768 the town chose not to dip into them when a new schoolhouse was needed; rather, it instructed the school committee to appeal to the townsmen for land on which to build, and money to pay for the schoolhouse. When the appeal failed, nothing more was heard of the new schoolhouse.[45]

Though Connecticut law required only four towns to maintain grammar schools, small villages occasionally hired college graduates to teach in writing schools. Saybrook, Branford, Danbury, Windsor, Guilford, Stratford, and Norwich sometimes boasted Yale graduates for a few years, and Ashford offered Harvard-educated Henry Cary for at least a brief spell in 1741. Masters in several of these towns actually taught Latin scholars —about one-third of Shubael Breed's thirty Norwich boys studied Latin in 1782 and an indeterminate number of Danbury boys worked through grammar books.[46]

Indeed from 1765 on, Danbury maintained a full-fledged grammar school. Left £800 "lawful money" by Comfort Star on his death in 1763, it began one in 1765 under public control. Interest from the Star legacy, not taxes, financed the school, which was to instruct "children and youth in the various

44. New London Town Meeting Records, 1740–1789, pp. 22–33, and passim (paged in pencil), City Clerk's Office.

45. Ibid., pp. 26, 96, 262.

46. For Saybrook see F. B. Dexter, *Biographical Sketches of the Graduates of Yale College* (6 vols. New York, 1885–1919), *1,* 67; Branford, Dexter, *1,* 106–07; Windsor, Dexter, *1,* 238; Guilford, Dexter, *1,* 277, 283, 286; Stratford, Dexter, *1,* 324; Norwich, Shubael Breed to Mason F. Cogswell, Feb. 1782, Mason Cogswell Papers, Yale; Ashford, Ashford Town Meetings, Apr. 13, 1741, CSL; Danbury, Connecticut Towns MSS, Box 373, CHS.

branches of Good Literature and in the English, Greek and Lattain Languages and in vulgar Arithmetick." [47] As in many towns, the selectmen made all administrative decisions. Soon after receiving the Star money they loaned it out at "lawful interest" and a few years later moved the school into its own building from "the Town-House," a building the town had provided.[48] During the Revolution debtors of the school repaid their obligations in depreciated currency, with the result that its capital sank to slightly less than £500. Still the school remained healthy long after the Revolution.[49]

Even when Danbury is counted, the ratio of Connecticut towns keeping grammar schools to the total number of hundred-family towns never, except early in the century, approached that of Massachusetts. In 1700 there were thirty towns in Connecticut, seven of which probably had one hundred families.[50] Four—the county towns—maintained grammar masters. Population increased steadily until in 1756, the year of the first reliable census, Connecticut's towns of one hundred families numbered at least fifty. Only four grammar schools were constantly maintained in this year. Eighteen years later at least sixty-eight towns counted one hundred families; but grammar schools still numbered only four.[51]

When the eighteenth-century opened, New Hampshire could count four less grammar schools than Connecticut—that is to say, none.

Separated from Massachusetts in 1679, it did not shake off many laws and traditions of the older colony, but it did permit the educational obligations of the statute of 1647 to lapse. The hundred-family requirement was unreasonable, New Hampshire towns seem to have believed. And they had good reasons

47. Conn. Towns MSS, Box 373.
48. Ibid.
49. Ibid.
50. Figures based on my own calculations from information given by Greene and Harrington, *American Population*.
51. Ibid., passim.

to think so: Indians threatened many towns; money for any public expense was hard to come by; and Harvard graduates were reluctant to give up livelier towns in Massachusetts for the quiet provincialism of New Hampshire villages.

By the late seventeenth century these reasons seemed less compelling, and in 1693 the General Court approved a bill requiring every town to provide a schoolmaster.[52] Since the statute failed to specify how long each year the master was to teach and since it did not require that he know Latin, no great burden was placed on town revenue. For the next fifteen years—until 1708—no town consistently maintained a grammar master if indeed any town hired one at all.[53]

By 1708 the lack of such a master was felt so acutely that the General Court decided that the province should have at least one school in which the languages might be studied. The school, the court determined, should be in Portsmouth. That town, with four other leading communities in the colony, would have to bear the cost. They could collect tuition from parents if they liked, or put the whole thing on the rates, but in some way they had to come up with fifty pounds every year for the master. To stimulate zeal for tax collection among the selectmen of these towns, a statute was drawn to include a provision which made them personally liable for any sum not raised. And in what was to have been a galling provision to the selectmen, the act provided that the Governor, Council, and "Settled ministers" of Portsmouth were to choose the master.[54]

The act was successful—a grammar school opened shortly after its passage, and stayed open throughout the life of the act. In 1717 the statute terminated and with it the school. But not for long. Shortly afterward Portsmouth found itself presented in court for failure to observe the requirement that every town maintain a master. This was intolerable to citizens of the town,

52. Batchellor, *Laws of New Hampshire*, 1, 560–61.
53. Ibid., 2, 85.
54. The statute is in ibid., 2, 85–86. The contributing towns were Hampton, Dover, Exeter, and Newcastle.

who protested and then, to end the embarrassment, dipped into
their own resources to maintain a grammar school. This time
the school took root, and thrived for the remainder of our
period.[55]

The draftsmen of the statute of 1708 may have hoped it
would irritate the contributing towns so much that each one
would found a school of its own. The act, after all, contained
an obvious injustice. It forced four towns to contribute to a
school which their children could attend only at great incon-
venience and expense. All the towns must have resented paying
the toll, but only one, Hampton, sought a way out by hiring
its own grammar master in 1714. The General Court, on learning of Hampton's action, freed the town of responsibility of any
further expense connected with the Portsmouth school.[56]

Since Hampton's example failed to inspire others to similar
action, the General Court turned once more to compulsion. In
a statute passed in 1719 (closely patterned on the old Massachusetts law), it ordered towns of fifty families to maintain a
writing master and those of one hundred families, a grammar
master. Like the Massachusetts act, the statute ordered the courts
to enforce the requirements—empowering the Quarter Sessions
of the Peace to collect fines up to twenty pounds for delinquency. The Massachusetts act did not explicitly provide a way
for towns which felt unable to comply to escape its requirement,
but the New Hampshire statute ordered the Quarter Sessions to
hear appeals from towns that believed themselves unable to live
up to the law.[57]

The act was never an unqualified success. Two years after its
passage so many hundred-family towns had ignored its requirements that the General Court amended it, making selectmen
liable to fines up to twenty pounds for only one month's neglect. Most of the failures probably derived from excessive thrift,

55. Ibid., 2, 98, 253, 651. Portsmouth Town Records, New Hampshire State Library.
56. Nathaniel Bouton et al., eds., *Documents and Records Relating to the Province
[Towns and State] of New Hampshire* (39 vols. Concord, 1867–1941), 3, 570.
57. Batchellor, 2, 336–37.

but a number stemmed from better causes. Dover, for example, like a number of New Hampshire towns located on the edge of the wilderness, faced attacks from the Indians in 1722, and its children coming from scattered houses to the school were in danger. This situation prompted the General Court to approve the suspension of education there during the war.[58] It also listened sympathetically to Londonderry in 1727, when that town pleaded its "infancy" (which apparently was equated with poverty) in defense of closing the school.[59]

Later in the century—in a safer and more prosperous time, the law was only imperfectly observed. New Hampshire was never a rich province and its citizens always hesitated to increase public expenditures. Town meetings frequently exhibited this concern. In the 1760s, for example, Barrington frequently refused to support any schools—or voted to maintain them for only two or three months in a year.[60] Education in Barrington, and in many other towns, came to be irregular and unpredictable. One year a master would be hired for ten months, the next two months, or perhaps not at all. The courts were aware of this bad performance and sometimes acted to improve it. But they, too, seem to have lacked sustained energies. Had they insisted on faithful observance of the law, about forty grammar schools would have been in existence when the Revolution began. As it was, though schools were regularly maintained at Portsmouth, Exeter, and a few other towns, only about half the required number of schools were meeting in 1775.[61]

Historians usually mark down the educational efforts of Rhode Island as negligible compared to those of Connecticut and Massachusetts. Samuel Eliot Morison tells us that in the

58. Bouton, 9, 155–56.
59. Ibid., 4, 268.
60. Barrington Town Records, New Hampshire State Library. See, for example, the meetings of the 1760s.
61. I have calculated the number of schools required by law from figures in Greene and Harrington. To determine the number in existence in 1775, I examined the Town Records in the New Hampshire State Library.

seventeenth century only one boy from Rhode Island attended college. In the next century additional youths from the small colony traveled to Harvard and Yale, but no college took shape in Rhode Island itself until just before the Revolution. As for education below the college level, the suspicions entertained by Rhode Islanders against compulsion of any kind prevented them from passing laws compelling towns or parishes to maintain schools. Untroubled by provincial laws, many towns left the problem of providing schools up to private means, which often were not available. The result: neither public nor private schools opened. No wonder Morison dismisses the colony as a "cultural chasm"! [62]

Yet there were public-supported schools in Rhode Island, even a few that offered instruction in Latin and Greek. Most of them were in towns which had been transferred from Massachusetts to Rhode Island on the settlement of a boundary dispute in 1747. Thoroughly imbued with the educational tradition of Massachusetts, they probably never considered dropping their grammar schools on removal from the Bay Colony's jurisdiction. One of them, Bristol, while still a Massachusetts town had, like most such towns, hired masters from Harvard.[63] As a Rhode Island town its eagerness to find a grammar master led it in 1749 to press Robert Treat Paine, then a master in Lunenberg, to come to teach its boys and to name "your own price." If Paine agreed, he was also to receive the use of a horse, and his expenses to and from the town.[64] Paine refused, whereupon Bristol, its zeal for education still boiling, offered £300 "at least . . . and all the Best treatment." [65]

The old Rhode Island towns in contrast did little about public education. Warwick, one of the four original towns, ap-

62. Morison, *Intellectual Life*, p. 70.

63. Nathan Prince to Thomas Prince, Aug. 14, 1718, July 27, 1719, Miscellaneous MSS, Bound, MHS.

64. Joseph Greenleaf to Robert Treat Paine, Mar. 13, 1749/50, Robert Treat Paine Papers, MHS.

65. Jer[emiah?] Finney to Robert Treat Paine, Mar. 26, 1750, Robert Treat Paine Papers.

propriated exactly twenty pounds for schools between 1700 and 1783—ten pounds in 1729 and ten in 1736.[66] No town-supported master taught boys at any time during the colonial period.

Providence, larger and wealthier, stood somewhere between Warwick and Bristol in its performance. In the seventeenth century it does not seem to have provided a public school of any type, though in 1663 it did reserve one hundred acres of land and six of meadow for a school.[67] Early in the eighteenth century the town built or bought a schoolhouse, which it leased to private masters; but it rarely, if ever, maintained a school of its own in the building. Few of the private masters seem to have taught the languages; and the only surviving records of the Town School Committee, presumably appointed by the meeting, indicate that in 1754 the school contained only readers and spellers.[68]

In the 1760s Moses Brown of the great merchant family, leading a small group of citizens, succeeded in arousing public interest in town-supported schools. After agitation for a new school building—Brown and his group shrewdly focused attention on the concrete side of education first—the town in 1768 agreed to bear the major share of the expense of construction and, more importantly, to meet all expenses of instruction by a school rate. From the sale of the old schoolhouse and lot the town was to realize £200 5s. 6d., all of which was to be applied to the new building; in addition it promised £100 from the town treasury. This left £182 11s. 6d. to be raised by subscription. The proprietors, as Brown's group styled themselves, promised to take care of this amount. Soon after the town's act they engaged a contractor, and the new schoolhouse was

66. Warwick Town Meeting Records, Sept. 1, 1729, Nov. 29, 1736, Clerk's Office, Apponaug, R.I.

67. W. C. Pelkly, ed., *The Early Records of the Town of Providence* (21 vols. Providence, 1892–1915), 3, 35.

68. "Rules and Orders Appointed by the Committee of the Town School House," Mar. 1, 1754, Moses Brown Papers, Miscellaneous Volumes, 3, RIHS. William R. Staples, *Annals of the Town of Providence* (Providence, 1843), p. 495.

built, a handsome two-story brick building forty feet long and thirty feet wide, with a bell tower ten feet square at one end. Despite the ease of these first steps, trouble soon appeared: the proprietors lagged in paying the builder, and the town proved reluctant to tax itself annually in order to maintain masters. For the remainder of our period, the proprietors, who retained title to the second story, either hired masters or leased their part of the building to private masters. The fine new building had not spurred support of public education after all; instead it merely helped to perpetuate the old system of part public and part private contributions—with neither side fully committed to paying masters.[69]

69. "Copy of Town Votes," Dec. 2, 1767; School Committee Report, Dec. 2, 1767, Jan. 1, 1768; "Agreement with Hammon and Talent"; "Subscribers' List," Mar. 17, 1768—all in Moses Brown Papers, Miscellaneous Volumes, 3; and *Providence Gazette,* Sept. 22, 1764, Jan. 9, 1768, Oct. 7, 1775.

3. City Schools: Boston and Newport

LIKE the towns all over New England, Boston began as a village. But less than a century after the founding it had shaken off its early character and around the opening of the eighteenth century it differed strikingly from the typical village. It was larger, of course. At the opening of the eighteenth century the city could count 6,700 inhabitants; thirty years later, 13,000; and at the outbreak of the Revolution, 16,000. By far the largest number of Boston's people were middle class, a scrambled collection of small merchants, shopkeepers, skilled craftsmen, and professionals whose typical member was less conscious of his current social status than of the possibility for raising it.

Boston offered opportunities to men on the make: trading abroad could lead to fortunes; then, as now, the right marriage could open doors to social and economic success; appointment to important provincial office could elevate a man's status; and college education could prepare one for numerous attractive possibilities. The upper class may have frowned on such mobility, even though at any given time in the century many of its members had been recruited from a lower status. Despite the possibilities of entrance, the "better sort" were not numerous; a few great officials, a larger number of great merchants and landowners, the important clergy and other professionals made up its ranks. At the other extreme there were many mechanics and less skilled craftsmen; below them came the indentured servants and apprentices, and lowest of all, a small number of Negro slaves.[1]

1. Carl Bridenbaugh, *Cities in the Wilderness, The First Century of Urban Life in*

The economic activities of these groups varied widely from those of the countryside. For throughout the colonial period Boston was the greatest port in New England, with lines of trade extending all over the Atlantic and into the Mediterranean. Its economic power also reached into the countryside, where its merchants looked for marketable commodities and sold imported goods of all sorts. Commerce reigned within the city, too. Shopkeepers hawked exotic and domestic products side by side; craftsmen made furniture, silver, and a host of other things and often combined shopkeeping with craftsmanship.[2]

Urban and commercial Boston bristled with problems. With its wooden buildings huddled together in huge clusters cut by narrow streets, the city needed fire protection on a scale unknown to the village. Its sanitation problems in an unsanitary age were immense. Poor relief tapped the city treasury every year. Commerce, Boston found, inevitably brought sailors and other transients, who patronized bawdy houses thinly disguised as taverns. All these problems were met more or less successfully (though the city never succeeded in banishing sailors or whores): fire watches and even fire engines were provided; regulations concerning refuse disposal were passed and enforced; overseers of the poor regularly provided food and care for Boston's unfortunate; and police protection eliminated or controlled many criminals.[3]

Long before the appearance of urban problems, Boston recognized the need for education and acted to provide it. By 1643 its town meeting had agreed to support a grammar school for local boys. In 1684 the city founded the Queen Street Writing School for smaller children and in 1700 the North Writing School. Thirteen years later, to satisfy parents in the north end, it established the North Grammar School and, in 1720 in re-

America, 1675–1742 (New York, 1955), chaps. 1, 4. The population figures are on pp. 143 and 303; and in Cities in Revolt, 1743–1776 (New York, 1955), pp. 5, 216.

2. Cities in the Wilderness, chaps. 3, 6.

3. Ibid., chaps. 7, 11.

sponse to the needs of the opposite side of town, the South
Writing School. Thus by the end of the second decade in the
eighteenth century Boston had five public schools.[4]

Boston's citizens took satisfaction in their hierarchy of
schools. It was one in which the functions and the constituencies
of the two kinds of schools remained distinct. At the first level,
in the writing schools, young boys learned to read, write, and
cypher; at the next, in the grammar schools, their older brothers,
themselves graduates of the writing schools, studied Latin and
Greek. Altogether this "system" resembled the structure usually
found in an English city much more than it did the village's
educational effort.

As in the village, the Boston meeting relied upon an assortment of special committees to aid in the management of education, although the meeting itself probably held a tighter control over the schools than did most villages. Appropriations and
salaries invariably had to obtain meeting approval. Masters
sometimes had to win the approbation of a meeting, but usually
their selection was left up to a committee or to the selectmen.
Ordinarily these committees and the board of selectmen contained only a few notables and a sprinkling of college-educated
men.[5]

But the inspection committees which annually scrutinized
the schools after 1710 glittered with men of talent and education. Before that date inspection was casual and sporadic. A
selectman would drop by a school, perhaps question a few
students, and talk to the master. Apparently ministers also
visited occasionally—Cotton Mather resolved in 1699 to visit
Boston's schools and "speak such things both to the Teachers
and the Scholars, as they may all bee the better for!"[6]

In 1709 shortly after the death of Boston's great master,
Ezekiel Cheever, the meeting voted to make regular annual

    4. Ibid., pp. 121–22, 281. *Reports of the Record Commissioners of the City of Boston* (39 vols. Boston, 1876–1909), 8, 90.
    5. *Reports of the Record Commissioners*, 8, 29, 65–66, and passim.
    6. Cotton Mather, "Diary," W. C. Ford, ed., Mass. Hist. Soc., *Coll.*, 7 ser. 7 (1911–12), 304.

inspections for "the promoting of Diligence and good literature" in the schools.[7] The inspection group was to be composed of "Gentlemen, of Liberal Education Together with Some of the Revd Ministers of the Town."[8] Five notables—Waite Winthrop, Samuel Sewall, Elisha Cooke, Isaac Addington, and Thomas Brattle—were appointed in 1710 to be the first inspectors, but no minister was included. This ruffled the feelings of Increase Mather, who apparently let his displeasure at being left out be known. Hearing of it, Samuel Sewall, himself an inspector, decided to soothe the minister, but before he could approach Mather that worthy warned him off. "I have no Call to that Service," he wrote Sewall—but added that "the Ministers of the Town are the fittest persons in the World to be Visitors of the School."[9] Leaving them off the board of inspectors was "a great disrespect, and Contempt but upon (not me but) all the Ministers in Boston." So egregious was the town's mistake that it could not be expunged by a belated appointment of the ministers: "A Secondary call from T. B. &c I esteem as none at all." Nevertheless, Mather informed Sewall, he intended to go to the schoolhouse alone and in secret—for he was "not willing that anyone should goe with me (especially not any of the Visitors chosen by the Town.)"—and preach a sermon to the children. Sewall replied immediately that the town had not intended to "offend" the ministers and asked Mather's pardon for the unwitting slight. As for the sermon, it should be delivered on the visitation day—"your work will thereby be much more Beautifull, much more Honorable, much more profitable." Probably fully aware that Mather, despite his asseverations of indifference, was panting to join the inspectors, he ended with a lyric plea—"Boston of the Massachusetts invites you, calls you, Courts you."

The town meeting did not second Sewall's invitation, and Increase Mather probably carried out his resolve alone. The next year the same inspectors were chosen and again the minis-

7. *Reports of the Record Commissioners*, 8, 65–66.
8. Ibid.
9. Ibid.

ters were ignored. But in 1714 and for the following five years
the town granted them a place among the inspectors.[10] In 1720
the town dropped the old committee and placed responsibility
for annual inspection with the selectmen "and Such as they
Shall desire to Assist them.[11] The selectmen seem to have wanted
company, for they customarily asked all or some of the town's
ministers as well as other persons to accompany them on their
visits.[12]

There is no reason to ascribe the inclusion of the ministers to
Mather's ludicrous striving. Rather, the ministers were included
because they represented one of the most intelligent and best-
educated segments of the community. Their exclusion the first
year was certainly inadvertent, though their omission the second
year may have been a snub calculated to rebuff Increase Mather's
meddlesomeness. In any case, theirs never became the loudest
voice among the inspectors, and indeed the schools always remained under lay control.

In time the visitations took the form of a great ceremony.
Frequently the governor and his council were invited along
with other great Boston names—Hutchinson, Wendell, Winthrop—and when great men like Sir William Pepperell were
in town, they too were invited. At the two grammar schools
these august figures paraded in, greeted masters and students,
and settled down briefly to hear the pride of the town perform.
Although doubtless primed for weeks for this day of days, the
boys probably recited their Latin nervously—but apparently
always to the satisfaction of their listeners, whose own Latin was
usually rusty or nonexistent. Since visitations were hard work,
the group usually repaired to Mrs. Wardwell's or the Orange
Tree Tavern afterward for drink and dinner at the town's
expense.[13]

10. Though they were not listed with the inspectors of 1719/20, they probably
served. See *Reports of the Record Commissioners, 8,* 100, 109, 117, 124, 129, 136, 142.
11. Ibid., *8,* 151.
12. See, for example, ibid., *13,* 153.
13. Ibid., pp. 165, 176, 202, 302; *15,* 184, 348; *17,* 164.

From the yearly inspection, the town expected a report which like the visit soon came to fall into a prescribed form: a general statement ("the schools are under good regulation"), followed by the number of scholars attending for the year.[14] For more perceptive assessments of masters and schools, the town occasionally ordered the selectmen along to make special inquiries. These sometimes produced changes, as, for example, the dismissal of a writing-school master; but on the whole, the public schools operated for most of the late colonial period without criticism.

Because a large proportion of the funds for school support came out of tax revenues, Boston's schools escaped most problems of inflation during the first half of the eighteenth century. Since its resources were so much greater than any village's, it did not have to pay nearly the proportion of its revenue toward education that the village did—even though it maintained five schools. Nevertheless, the town did expend significant sums on schools. What income was obtained from investments in land belonging to the schools cannot be known, but apparently it was not large.[15]

The figures for the period beginning with the middle of the century are the most complete of all. In 1750 the total town charges were £4,000 lawful money; during the year the treasurer paid £670 in masters' salaries—the largest part of school expenses in any year and probably the only expenditure in some. Of the £670, almost half, £290, went to the two grammar-school masters and the usher of the South Grammar School. Ten years later Boston's total expenditures came to £4,500, £760 of which was for the salaries of masters; and in 1770, £4,000, of which £630 was for schools. The percentages remained fairly constant: about 16 per cent of the town's total charges was paid to schools.[16]

Only occasionally do there seem to have been open com-

14. Ibid., *12*, 246. For similar reports see *12*, 265, 291–92; *14*, 215–16.
15. For school lands see ibid., *13*, 77, 90, 146.
16. Ibid., *14*, 177; *16*, 42; *18*, 26.

plaints about the size of expenditures for public education. In
1751 several inhabitants petitioned the town to "Consider of
the great Expence occasion'd by the Public Schools" and suggested that a single grammar school instead of two, and two
writing schools in place of three, would prove "sufficient for
the Education of the Children of the Town." [17] Although the
petition was withdrawn the same day it was presented, the
meeting appointed a committee to examine the causes of the
great annual expenses of the town.[18]

This committee's report, given two months later, reaffirmed
Boston's commitment to its costly school system. Admitting
that the schools were not cheap, indeed that one-third of the
selectmen's expenditures of the previous year which went for
the schools was a "very Considerable sum," the committee concluded that no cuts could be made unless the town forced parents of attending children to contribute. The implication of
the report was evident: the town could afford the cost, for, as
the report stated, "the Education of Children is of the greatest
Importance to the Community." [19]

In Newport as in Boston, size, social complexity, and commerce were the stuff of urban affairs. But Newport for all its
surface similarities to the Bay city was not Boston. At the opening of the eighteenth century its 2,600 inhabitants amounted
to a little more than one-third of Boston's; in 1730 the ratio
was about the same, 4,640 people in Newport to 13,000 in Boston; and though by the beginning of the Revolution Newport's
population had gained, its 11,000 still fell 5,000 short of
Boston's.[20]

Commercially, Newport never managed to equal Boston. It
did ease into the coastal trade, long the domain of Boston's mer-

17. Ibid., *14*, 187–88.
18. Ibid., p. 192.
19. Ibid., p. 197.
20. Bridenbaugh, *Cities in the Wilderness*, pp. 143, 303. *Cities in Revolt*, pp. 53,
216.

chants, and even into the older city's inland exchange with Connecticut and southern Massachusetts. At the same time, Newport remained more or less dependent upon Boston for its manufactured goods, though by 1730 its own energetic crafts-men turned out hats, furniture, and ships.[21]

Newport's class structure resembled Boston's, though its upper class was more narrowly mercantile. The other classes also reflected the city's close ties to the sea: for example, young men of Newport went to sea, though the scarcity of land in Rhode Island may have been as important as the demands of commerce in their choice of occupations. The pull of ocean commerce upon white labor may also have led to the importa-tion of many Negro slaves; in any case the city grew more and more dependent upon them.[22]

Despite its autonomy (bestowed upon it early in the eight-eenth century by the General Assembly) and geographical isolation from the rest of Rhode Island, Newport did not escape the inflation and the currency depreciation that troubled the colony for much of the eighteenth century. Nor was the city entirely free from political problems. In 1741 the "Woods Part" north of its center petitioned to be set off as a separate town. Newport's citizens, loath to lose the rates contributed by the Woods' people, resisted the division; but it came anyway in 1743 when the Assembly incorporated the northern section as Middletown.[23]

Newport lacked another sort of cohesion, too. In a day in which a single church denomination often provided a center of life, Newport contained three or four large religious groups. At the opening of the century fully half of its people were Quakers. There was also a large contingent of Baptists, and the Episcopalians were on the increase. Though the Congrega-tionalists did not form a church until 1720, they too gradually added to their number. Moravians and other groups also mi-

21. Bridenbaugh, *Cities in the Wilderness*, chaps. 2, 6, 10.
22. Ibid.
23. Ibid., p. 305.

grated to Newport. This religious diversity marked Newport throughout the eighteenth century.[24]

More than inflation, unstable currency, and occasional political divisions, sectarianism left its impress upon education in Newport. Impelled by a determination to preserve its identity, every important denomination spent its resources on its own children. Most exclusive of all were the Friends, who established a school to keep their children free of the town schools "where they are Taught the corrupt ways, manners, fashions and Tongue of the world." [25] Though such intense separatism inspirited the Friends alone, other sects also set up their own schools: the Congregationalists and Baptists in 1729, Episcopalians in 1741, and Moravians in 1772.[26]

Had these religious groups shared the convictions of the Friends that contamination lurked in public schools, none would have been possible. They did not, and Newport provided public schools. Still, church efforts drew attention from the town's schools as the meager references to them in the town records show, and tapped the funds that might otherwise have been available.

With the money at its disposal, the town rarely paid masters' salaries out of tax revenues. Instead it relied upon income from lands set aside for the support of schools, a fairly common practice in other towns as we have seen. How much land Newport designated for schools and how much individuals donated cannot be determined from the town records. Nor can the arrangements made in the early eighteenth century to exploit these lands be discovered. Probably both long and short term leases were given. In any case in 1763 a committee appointed by the town divided the school holdings into small lots for long term leasing—on which an annual rent was to be paid.

24. Ibid., pp. 263–64, 419–20.
25. Quoted ibid., p. 285.
26. Ibid., pp. 445–46. Ezra Stiles, *The Literary Diary*, ed. F. B. Dexter (3 vols. New York, 1901), *1*, 159.

An undetermined number of these lots were leased and rent on them collected every year. But not all could be disposed of immediately, for the town advertised them as late as 1774.[27]

Since the schools' endowment did not yield sufficient income to meet all expenses and since church efforts scanted the town's, Newport had no choice but to collect tuition from parents. This prevented some children of the poor from attending, though the town made several efforts to encourage their education. As for children who threatened to become a charge on the town, the overseers could always bind them out and periodically did so.[28]

For the public grammar school the consequences of Newport's diffuse efforts are clear. In 1700 James Galloway began to teach Latin in the town schoolhouse, though he was not in the town's pay, and in fact only rented several rooms from the town for his school.[29] Until 1720 the town school only irregularly housed a Latin master, and when it did he seems always to have paid his own way. But from 1720 until 1774 Newport fairly consistently hired a master capable of giving a grammar education. Yet in many years the records say nothing about him or his school, and in most years the town raised his salary not from taxes but from school land rent and tuition payments. Time did not increase Newport's commitment to its grammar school: as late as 1775 the schoolhouse seems to have been put up for lease.[30]

When the school was in session, its supervision fell to committees irregularly appointed and apparently irregularly active. There seems to have been neither an annual inspection nor a report to the meeting.

Located in a colony which did not compel towns to maintain schools, Newport never fully convinced itself that educa-

27. Newport Town Meeting Records (1741–1776), p. 214, Newport Historical Society. *Newport Mercury*, Mar. 28, 1774.
28. Newport Town Meeting Records (1741–1776), p. 179.
29. Ibid. (1682–1739), p. 145.
30. Ibid. (1741–1776), p. 377.

tion should be a public responsibility. At times it opened the grammar school, but conviction weakened and the school soon reverted to a status more private than public. Where the close-knit Boston community was deeply committed to an educational purpose and able to carry it out, Newport, more tolerant, more cosmopolitan, but less cohesive, was unable to develop or to sustain a school system adequate to its needs.

4 The Development
of Private Education

ON September 25, 1769, William Rogers, a graduate of Rhode Island College's first class a scant eighteen days before, opened a grammar school in Newport. The school was not entirely his own idea. Before it began, "several Gentlemen" of the city gave him "great Encouragement" and promised that "they will forward as much as Possible such a laudable Undertaking." [1] Their encouragement may have included opening their purses to Rogers, for his scholars numbered only three on opening day, although if so, not to the extent of supplying the Latin grammars which his scholars so badly needed. But neither money nor books worried him. The first he expected to collect from his scholars; and for Latin grammars, he begged of his friends, purchased of a townswoman, and waited patiently for a shipment from New York. For a classroom he seems to have used his chamber in a private home. [2]

In this manner Rogers got his school under way. Short of books and scholars, meeting in a private house, it was, like hundreds of others begun in the eighteenth century, a simple affair. No public agency participated in its founding, managed its income, or inspected its scholars. In Massachusetts a private master did have to convince the selectmen of his town that he was qualified to teach, and if he gave instruction in the languages he had to submit like his brothers in public grammar

1. William Rogers to David Howell, Sept. 26, 1769, Brown University Miscellaneous Papers, Brown University Library.
2. Ibid. *Newport Mercury*, Oct. 9, 1769.

schools to an examination by the local ministers. Afterward
he was on his own.[3]

On the surface the situation of a private master was a happy
one: he apparently taught what he pleased, fixed his own hours
of instruction, limited the number of scholars if he chose,
selected the classroom, and in other ways controlled his daily
routine. In practice he was not so free. He usually taught in
his own chamber because no other place was so cheap; he accepted all comers in order to make a profit; his hours often depended upon his scholars' convenience; and the curriculum had
to be shaped to the demand. Indeed, despite its apparent freedom from external control, the private school no less than the
public one had to be responsive to its constituency.

Private schools offered a bewildering variety of subjects.
Though no two curricula were quite alike, the subjects taught
fell into two broad categories—"academical" and "useful," as
the eighteenth century called them. Latin and Greek, logic,
rhetoric, English grammar, and sometimes mathematics, natural
philosophy, astronomy, and geography were academical, while
bookkeeping, surveying, navigation, gauging, mensuration,
shorthand, and other vocational subjects were useful. The line
between the two classifications shifted with the person drawing
it, and in some schools subjects from both categories appeared
together. Solomon Porter of East Windsor taught such a school
in the early 1780s. When he began teaching soon after his
graduation from Yale in 1775 he seems to have confined his
school to Latin and Greek, and perhaps reading and writing.
But by 1783 his curriculum also included mathematics, geography, trigonometry, surveying, sailing, and English grammar.[4]

Though masters with Porter's flexibility, or ambition, were
not rare, most tended to specialize in either vocational or
academical subjects. Those giving vocational training sought
the cities and large towns where people were increasingly interested in business growth.

3. *Acts and Resolves*, 1, 470.
4. Ebenezer Baldwin to Solomon Porter, Sept. 13, 1776, Baldwin Family Papers,
Yale. *Connecticut Courant*, Apr. 1783.

Leading the economic advance, of course, was commercial Boston, which needed young men with technical education—navigators to chart the courses of its wandering ships, surveyors to lay out lands bought by its prosperous merchants, bookkeepers and scribes to keep the records of countinghouses and shops, and others to help handle the city's proliferating business. In search of these skills no one turned to the city's public schools; their limited functions were well known and approved. Instead one searched out a private master, who usually announced his availability in a local newspaper.

Some Boston masters undertook to board their charges as well as to instruct them. But since boys from out of town were in the minority, ordinarily a master did not attempt to combine housekeeping with education. Instead he set off a part of his own living space, collected what books, paper, and instruments he needed, and advertised the broad range of his knowledge—provided, of course, that the Boston selectmen approved his undertaking.[5]

Enough masters satisfied the selectmen to present a variety of instruction in the city. For business training early in the century a boy could practice drawing bonds, bills, and indentures under the tutelage of John Green.[6] In 1728 ambitious lads could learn the intricacies of shorthand from Caleb Philips, who taught a "way of Joyning, 3, 4, 5, & 6 words in one in every Sentence by the Moods, Tenses, Persons, and Verb." [7] Philips came highly recommended by six Boston ministers who, not realizing the possibilities shorthand held for easing the work of clerks and scribes, recommended Philips' shorthand "especially to Scholars, and those that would preserve the Sermons they hear in public for their further and lasting use." [8] Training that enabled a scribe to cope with his minister's words and his employer's letters and accounts was convenient indeed! Most youths looking to business for a living probably settled for

5. The licensing act passed in 1711/12 is in *Acts and Resolves*, 1, 681–82.
6. *Boston News-Letter*, Mar. 28, 1708/09.
7. *Boston Gazette*, Mar. 25, 1728.
8. Ibid., Apr. 8, 1728.

straightforward bookkeeping and merchants' accounting, which were offered throughout the colonial period.

If a boy rebelled at the prospect of a stuffy countinghouse and persuaded his father that a career at sea or out of doors would be more profitable, he might prepare himself by studying navigation or surveying with one of Boston's many instructors. Owen Harris taught both in 1709—and probably for the next fifty years—along with writing, arithmetic, geometry, trigonometry, dialing, gauging, and astronomy. In addition he offered instruction in "the Projection of the Sphaere, and the use of Mathematical Instruments." [9] This was not an unusual list of subjects taken together; a master who taught navigation would also train surveyors; and, since both subjects required it, trigonometry and other simpler branches of mathematics would be offered. Though Harris' advertisement did not mention algebra, he probably taught it, but if he did not, others did. [10]

Only occasionally did masters who gave instruction in navigation, surveying, and mathematics also teach bookkeeping and other business subjects. Joseph Kent probably did in 1737, and Richard Green combined them in 1757. [11] But usually a boy who wished to sample all sorts of practical courses had to go to more than one master.

Doubtless few boys completely mastered these subjects before they had to go to work; but if they did and hungered for higher mathematics, they were out of luck. Isaac Greenwood, the first Hollis Professor of Mathematics at Harvard did teach the calculus and "Branches of NATURAL PHILOSOPHY, as Mechanics, Optics, [and] Astronomy" for about a year in 1738 and 1739; but since his uncontrollable fondness for liquor had cost him his chair in the College in 1738, most parents probably were reluctant to trust their sons to his care. The unfortunate Greenwood soon closed his school and departed for Philadel-

9. *Boston News-Letter*, Mar. 21, 1708/09.
10. *Boston Gazette*, Mar. 26, 1720.
11. *Boston Weekly News-Letter*, June 30, 1737. *Boston Gazette*, Sept. 19, 1757.

phia.[12] Four years later Nathan Prince, another bibulous instructor banished from Harvard, opened one. He offered the usual subjects—geometry, algebra, trigonometry, navigation, surveying, geography, astronomy, gauging and dialing—besides two unusual ones, fortifications and gunnery. Prince also proposed to give lectures on history and natural philosophy. Although his intellectual reputation was great, he could not make a success of his school—probably because he was known to be cantankerous when drunk.[13]

There were few vocational schools outside Boston and Newport until around 1750. By that date six or eight towns had achieved some commercial importance and consequently required young men trained for business. Teachers of bookkeeping, navigation, and other "useful" subjects soon appeared. In New Haven, for example, John Miller taught navigation in 1769; and in nearby New London during the following year Cornelius Conohan gave instruction in bookkeeping "according to the Italian Method." Similar schools existed in Providence, Salem, Hartford, and several smaller towns.[14]

In contrast to their colleagues who concentrated on vocational training and who consequently were bound to the cities and large towns, masters who limited their teaching to the languages and mathematics discovered opportunities in small as well as large towns. In part their spread resulted from the desire of organized groups in towns lacking schools to give classical training to their sons—groups, for example, like the one which had encouraged William Rogers in Newport—but a few taught in towns which also had public-supported Latin schools.[15]

12. *Boston Gazette*, April 2, 1739. *Boston Weekly News-Letter*, Nov. 9, 1738. Shipton, *Biographical Sketches*, 6, 479.

13. *Boston Weekly News-Letter*, Mar. 3, 1742/43.

14. *Connecticut Journal*, May 27, 1768. *New London Gazette*, July 20, 1770. *Providence Gazette*, Sept. 12, 1772, Feb. 12, 1774. *Essex Gazette*, Sept. 28, 1773. *Connecticut Courant*, May 13, 1783.

15. Westfield, Mass., for example. See Journal of John Ballantine, May 12, 1770, May 14, 1770, AAS.

A few sponsors took more of a hand in the management of their schools than Rogers had. The gentlemen who invited Enoch Perkins to teach Latin and Greek at Newport in 1781 evidently secured a room for his class in the city's new State House and may also have found him a place to live. No doubt they saw to it that the school was well attended. In any case boys came in such gratifying numbers that Perkins, who in August shortly after his arrival had declared his "prospects tolerable, or what you may call middling good," by November exulted that "the profits will be something handsome." [16] With the school well launched, full control fell into his hands and nothing more was heard of his backers. He continued happily in his school for two years, but gave it up for a career at the bar.[17]

An entirely different case is presented by New London's Union School, established in 1773 by twelve citizens including Richard Law, a graduate of Yale and the town's leading attorney. It soon had its own building and a charter of incorporation issued by the legislature in 1774. The charter placed full governing power in the hands of the original proprietors, who were allowed full corporate powers. For the school the fact that it had a charter guaranteed a measure of permanence which was more important than the specific terms of incorporation. The proprietors imposed a business-like routine on school affairs: the master was hired after a meticulous inquiry into his background; he was paid quarterly; and, most important, he taught only Latin, Greek, and mathematics and could leave to the proprietors the day-to-day problems of keeping the schoolhouse in repair.[18]

At the time the proprietors of the Union School first met,

16. Enoch Perkins to Simeon Baldwin, Aug. 4, 1781, Nov. 30, 1781, Baldwin Family Papers. *Newport Mercury*, July 28, 1781.

17. For Perkins' later career see Dexter, *Biographical Sketches of the Graduates of Yale, 4*, 199–200.

18. MSS Notice of Proprietors' Meeting, Nov. 23, 1774, in Connecticut Towns, Box 378, CHS. Trumbull and Hoadly, *Public Records of the Colony of Conn., 14*, 382–84. *New London Gazette*, Dec. 10, 1773, May 10, 1778.

a different kind of grammar school flourished in Providence. As in the Union School its curriculum was classical but Rhode Island College, not a group of private citizens, sponsored it. It had opened in Warren in 1764 under James Manning three years before the College began. When Manning undertook the College, he continued to meet his grammar school; its scholars in fact sat beside those of the College in the Warren parsonage. The grammar school accompanied the College when it moved to Providence in 1770; and two years later both removed to the new College building. The move brought scholars and the scholars brought prosperity. In 1776 these boys, who had numbered eighteen two years before, enjoyed one hour of instruction a day in a writing school which had recently been added to the College. College and school closed with the Revolution, but both opened again in 1780. And though in 1782 the school instructed only eleven scholars, it evidently was in full operation once more.[19]

During this period the College Corporation permitted President Manning to run the grammar school in his own way. No official action regarding the school appears in the Corporation Records, though Corporation minutes of November and December 1782 refer to it as 'anexed to the Colledge." [20] The school's master—President Manning did the job part of the time—received no compensation from the Corporation, presumably relying on tuition payments for his income. Even though the Corporation paid nothing, the school benefited from its connection to the College, for it received a room in the College building and it drew boys who wished to prepare for entrance into the freshman class.[21]

19. Corporation Committee to Moses Lindo, Jan. 1, 1771, Brown Univ., Miscellaneous Papers. Description of College, Jan. 1774?, Brown, Miscellaneous Papers. *Providence Gazette,* Mar. 9, 30, 1776, May 4, 1776. MSS Advertisement, Brown, Miscellaneous Papers, April 13, 1780. "Estimate for the College," Nov. 27, 1782, Brown, Miscellaneous Papers. Walter C. Bronson, *The History of Brown* (Providence, 1914), p. 58.
20. Brown Univ., Miscellaneous Papers.
21. I have searched the Brown Corporation Records carefully; the Brown Univ. Miscellaneous Papers contain much on the school.

Though many private grammar schools were the creation of private groups, many more were established by the masters themselves without any outside encouragement. Most closed after two or three years, not for lack of support but because their masters gave them up, having founded them simply to earn temporary livings while preparing for careers in other fields. An occasional one lasted much longer: for example, after he gave up the Braintree town school in 1743, Joseph Marsh conducted a private school for eighteen years in the old parsonage, which he shared with his mother and sister.[22] Daniel Wadsworth's school in Farmington, Connecticut, in the late 1720s was representative of a greater number of schools, lasting only the two or three years it took him to prepare for the pulpit.[23]

Ministers probably prepared more boys for college than all other private masters combined. Those who taught for a number of years gradually built their reputations in the classroom as well as in the pulpit and attracted boys from near and far. Since boys from out of town usually boarded where they learned, ministers picked up extra income from them. Few equaled the enterprise of the Reverend John Ballantine of Westfield, Massachusetts, who not only boarded his scholars but also put them to work picking corn in his fields when they were not studying their grammar.[24]

Private schools, like public, usually catered exclusively to boys, but some accepted girls part time or at odd hours. A few like Ebenezer Dayton's in Newport allowed girls to attend during regular hours, but Dayton separated the two sexes—boys in one room and girls in another.[25] The more usual arrangement was to have girls come early in the morning for a couple of

22. Shipton, *Biographical Sketches*, 8, 448–49.

23. Daniel Wadsworth Diary, CHS.

24. Journal of John Ballantine, Oct. 11, 1773. For other ministers who taught see Shipton, *4*, 98; *5*, 15, 30.

25. *Newport Mercury*, Mar. 6, 1769.

hours, say from six until eight o'clock, when the pampered boys—presumably well-rested after their two extra hours of sleep—arrived. Around four in the afternoon, when the boys left for the day, the girls returned for a final two hours.[26]

Tired masters must have wondered—especially at six in the morning—if keeping boys and girls apart was really important. In reflective moments they knew that a moral imperative decreed that the sexes be separated: to avoid temptation, it held, do not teach boys and girls together. Practically, too, there was good reason to teach girls by themselves. Their curriculum hardly suited boys, who attended school for different purposes. Only a resourceful master could have juggled the two curricula at the same time in the same room. Most masters did not try.[27]

Education for the girl of an ordinary middle-class family meant reading, writing, perhaps simple arithmetic, and, above all else, sewing (which, of course, she learned from a schoolmistress). If her parents aspired to gentility, she might also learn French, study English grammar and composition, and read a little geography and history. But only a girl with enlightened parents ever went this far.[28]

Early in the eighteenth century schools providing this amount of education for girls were scarce. Boston had the greatest number, but even in Boston their number in any given year was not large and in many years there were none at all. Frequently these schools boarded their charges, a service intended to attract girls from outside the city, for most Boston girls lived at home where their parents could keep an eye on them.[29]

Like Boston, Newport supported several private girls' schools during the colonial period. Mrs. Sarah Osborn kept one, which enjoyed an exceptionally long life. Starting in the 1730s, Mrs.

26. Master Ebenezer Bradford of Newport kept a school during these hours in 1769: ibid., July 17, 1769.

27. *New London Gazette*, Mar. 20, 1772. *Connecticut Journal*, Oct. 22, 1783.

28. Ibid. *Essex Gazette*, Apr. 20, 1773. *Newport Mercury*, Dec. 19, 1758.

29. *Boston News-Letter*, Sept. 9, 1706, Apr. 7, 1761.

Osborn taught steadily for more than thirty years. With a
large family herself, she boarded eight or ten of her students
a year and instructed as many as seventy girls at a time. These
girls came to her from all over New England to learn to read,
write, and sew. They also received daily religious instruction,
for Mrs. Osborn was zealous in promoting "the good of
souls." [30]

Outside Boston and Newport only the large towns had the
wealth and population to support girls' schools, and many of
these had to seek scholars from near and far to remain open.
One such Salem school in 1774 lured girls into its classroom
by offering not only to teach them many of the customary subjects but also to introduce them "into genteel Company, all at a
moderate Expence." [31] Other schools could not match this proposal, but another one in Salem boasted that its teaching was
accomplished with the "best, newest, and genteelest Methods
now in Use." [32]

With a teaching staff of one—usually a woman who worried over her girls' morals as much as their minds—these schools
were small. But besides lone women instructors, an occasional
married pair earned the family living by maintaining a school.
John Druitt and his wife Eleanor of Boston were such a couple:
John in 1773 taught reading, writing, arithmetic, and "Or-
thography," and Eleanor gave instruction in French and sewing. The following year they rearranged the subjects. John now
offered English, letter writing, and arithmetic; Eleanor added
reading and spelling to the French and needlework she had
taught the previous year.[33]

Women instructors frequently ran small millinery shops
while they taught; the connection between teaching and millinery was natural, since the principal part of the typical cur-

30. Samuel Hopkins, *Memoirs of the Life of Mrs. Sarah Osborn* (Worcester, Mass.,
1799), pp. 59–60; the quotation is from her Diary, entry given on p. 61. See also
Newport Mercury, Dec. 19, 1758.

31. *Essex Gazette*, July 19, 1774.

32. Ibid., Apr. 20, 1773.

33. *Boston Weekly News-Letter*, Apr. 1, 1773, Apr. 28, 1774.

riculum was sewing. One of the most successful must have been Mrs. Jane Day of Boston, who maintained a boarding school for at least eight years and who also made women's dresses "in the newest Fashion." [34] Salem's Elizabeth Gaudin, an equally enterprizing teacher, sold ribbon, silk, pins, and needles when she was not in the classroom.[35]

The dressmaking of Jane Day and the shopkeeping of Elizabeth Gaudin hint that private mistresses did not find the financial rewards of teaching high. Nor for that matter did masters who sometimes combined teaching with bookkeeping or other jobs. Tuition supplied their incomes and tuition could not be high if students were to be attracted.

There are few figures for the pre-Revolutionary period but it seems unlikely that tuition amounted to as much as a shilling a week in most vocational schools anytime before 1783. Latin schools charged more. At the end of the seventeenth century Peter Burr, a Boston grammar master, received two pounds a year for each scholar, which probably equaled about one shilling a week when vacation time is subtracted from the calendar year.[36] By 1768 tuition for Latin scholars in Boston had increased, if Master Theophilus Chamberlain's prices are representative. Chamberlain collected "one Guinea per Quarter" for each scholar, a rate of more than a shilling and a half per week.[37]

Tuition charges for girls varied widely with the subjects given. Little Sarah Hutchinson of Boston attended Mrs. Trivet's school for four pence per week, probably receiving instruction in the usual reading, writing, and needlework.[38] Music and dancing would have raised these charges considerably. In 1720

34. *Newport Mercury*, May 8, 1759. (Boston teachers often advertised in the Newport and Providence papers.)

35. *Essex Gazette*, Apr. 27, 1773.

36. Peter Burr Commonplace Book, MHS.

37. *Boston Chronicle*, Sept. 5, 1768.

38. Peter Orlando Hutchinson, comp., *The Diary and Letters of Thomas Hutchinson* (2 vols. London, 1883–86), I, 41.

Edward Enstone's school, which gave lessons in these subjects besides sewing, collected one pound at entrance and two pounds per quarter.[39] Boarding schools also were expensive: in 1769 Mary Speakman in Marlborough opened one which instructed girls in reading and needlework for eight shillings (lawful money) per week.[40]

Parents met all the charges of private education. In the two cities and the large towns the sum of these charges was large, for vocational schools grew in number throughout the colonial period. Private education thus freed public finances from a heavy burden. In relieving public education of the necessity of extending its scope, private schools had yet another effect: they helped confirm the traditional conception of the role of public-supported education. Classical learning in town schools surely would have encountered opposition had private schools not satisfied the demands of an expanding commerce. Thus though they served the most progressive impulses in the community, private schools had an impact that was also profoundly conservative.

39. *Boston Gazette*, Sept. 19, 1720.
40. *Massachusetts Gazette and Boston News-Letter*, June 22, 1769.

5. The Curriculum: Latin, Greek, Rhetoric, and Logic

AT the age of eighty-one, Colonel John Trumbull, painter of the Revolution's great, vividly remembered his boyhood triumph. As a six-year-old scholar in Master Nathan Tisdale's school in Lebanon, Connecticut, he had demonstrated his superior knowledge of Greek in a reading contest with an older boy: "We read the five verses of the Gospel of St. John; I missed not a word—he missed one, and I gained the victory." [1] Trumbull found even greater satisfaction in the reflection that his early years had provided a strenuous introduction to learning. He had begun Greek and Latin before he could have commanded English with any ease. At first he simply memorized like "a parrot" with little understanding of the words he read —grim work for a boy of six. In arithmetic the way was equally rocky. Early in his study a division problem puzzled him, but Master Tisdale refused to come to his aid, and the problem stayed on his slate until he solved it three months later. Through it all, he did not become discouraged but studied his language lessons diligently and solved most arithmetic problems in less than three months. [2]

When he entered Harvard at fifteen—three years after Tisdale declared him ready—Trumbull had read many volumes of history, was thoroughly prepared in geography, knew arithmetic, geometry, trigonometry, navigation, and surveying. In addition, he had read Eutropius, Cornelius Nepos, Virgil, Cicero,

---

1. Theodore Sizer, ed., *The Autobiography of Colonel John Trumbull, Patriot Artist, 1756–1843* (New Haven, 1953), p. 5.

2. Ibid., pp. 5, 9.

Horace, and Juvenal in Latin, and the New Testament and Homer's *Iliad* in Greek.[3]

The romanticism that infects the aged when youth is recalled may have led Trumbull to exaggerate the number of his accomplishments. Still, this impressive list evidently represented so much knowledge that the president and tutors of Harvard—who usually remained unimpressed even by the brightest scholars—admitted him as a junior.[4] Most of Trumbull's peers at Harvard, Yale, and the infant Rhode Island College entered with much less in their heads. A candidate's ability to read Latin and Greek, not his knowledge of navigation, surveying, history, or any of the other subjects Trumbull studied, interested the colleges.

Since grammar masters knew that colonial colleges required young scholars to display their knowledge of Latin and Greek, they exercised their charges in the classics—and little else. Naturally enough they concentrated on the works from which candidates for college admission were expected to recite. These varied little throughout most of the eighteenth century, for then as today college trustees were rarely given to change.[5]

The Harvard Laws of 1655 set the pattern. They stipulated that a scholar should be able to read "ordinary Classicall Authors," understand Greek grammar, speak or write Latin prose, and possess skill in writing Latin verse. Representative "ordinary" authors mentioned were Cicero and Virgil in Latin, and Isocrates and the New Testament in Greek.[6] Since the examiners sometimes presented candidates with passages from other authors, a wise youth did not stop with the ones listed in the Laws. In the next century the requirements changed but little, although after 1734 the examiners became insistent that candi-

3. Ibid., pp. 9–10.

4. Ibid., p. 10.

5. There are several accounts of entrance examinations; among them see L. H. Butterfield, ed., *The Adams Papers: Diary and Autobiography of John Adams* (4 vols. Cambridge, Mass., 1961), 3, 258–60.

6. "Harvard College Records, Part III," Col. Soc. of Mass., *Collections*, 31 (Boston, 1935), 329.

dates "be found Able . . . to write true Latin," and in 1767 Xenophon replaced Isocrates as an example of an ordinary Greek author.[7]

Yale and Rhode Island College followed the Harvard line almost exactly until 1745, when Yale added to the classics an understanding of "the Rules of . . . Common Arithmetic." [8] Rhode Island College adopted a similar requirement in 1783.[9]

Besides the classical authors they expected their scholars to meet in the examinations, masters frequently introduced others to their schools. Erasmus was studied almost as widely as Virgil ∩nd Cicero, and after them Ovid, Horace, and Homer were among the favorites. Others figured in the curriculum of many schools but, all in all, the range of authors was not wide. These few ancients, educated men seem to have agreed, offered the best of the classical world.[10]

Less agreement existed on the method of learning Latin. Some masters relied upon methods that were already old in the Middle Ages. Medieval teaching practices implied that if a boy was not a compound of memory and self-reliance, he should be. A boy in a fifteenth-century grammar school first memorized the rules of grammar in Latin. When he could recite a sufficient amount of grammar and came to reading, he faced new problems. His textbooks contained no English, and his master gave him little help beyond construing [11] aloud passages to be read— not in English, of course. The last resort was the dictionary.

7. "Harvard College Records, Part I," ibid., 15 (Boston, 1925), 134. A later statement of requirements is in an advertisement signed by President Edward Holyoke in *Boston News-Letter,* Sept. 5, 1745; see also ibid., Oct. 1, 1761. For the Xenophon requirement see "Harvard College Records, Part III," Col. Soc. of Mass., *Collections, 31,* 347.

8. Yale's requirements in 1726 are in Dexter, *Biographical Sketches of the Graduates of Yale College, 1,* 347; for the 1745 requirement see 2, 2.

9. Brown Corporation Records, 1, Pt. I, 90–91, Brown University Archives.

10. This is based on a variety of sources, including diaries, letters, newspapers, and textbooks cited below.

11. Construing a sentence meant analyzing the words in such an order as to reveal the meaning. Parsing, a similar exercise, meant breaking down a sentence into its parts of speech, describing each grammatically.

With its help a student was expected to learn by heart whole chunks of the classics, which he repeated on recitation days.[12]

In the sixteenth century, English ideas about teaching the languages began to shift, with Masters John Brinsley and Charles Hoole leading the way. Their new techniques prized a well-stocked memory as highly as did the old but suggested new ways of obtaining the nourishment. Scholars, the reformers urged, should "be taught to do all things with understanding," since they learned, and remembered, only if they really understood what they were about.[13] To ensure understanding, Hoole proposed that scholars be furnished textbooks containing English translations, and he himself prepared several which circulated widely.[14]

Yet so slowly did new ideas alter old practices that near the end of the seventeenth century John Locke complained of the persistence of the traditional command to memorize. Locke's own method of teaching Latin scorned the medieval emphasis on memory and grammar. From his sensationalist presumptions he deduced that the best way to learn Latin was one that approximated the way an English boy learned his own language. Let a tutor talk Latin into a boy, and if hiring a tutor proved impossible, the next best thing was to put the boy to reading in "some easy and pleasant Book, such as Aesops Fables," in which an English translation "made as literal as it can be" appeared line by line over the Latin. Keep him reading these lines "every Day over and over again, till he perfectly understands the *Latin,* and then go on to another." Above all, while he is learning to read, avoid troubling the scholar with questions about grammar, which is for adults and mature scholars. Young minds soon lose their bearings in rules of syntax and similar complexities. The

12. Foster Watson, *The Old Grammar Schools* (Cambridge, Eng., 1916), pp. 40–41. Baldwin, *William Shakspere's Small Latine and Lesse Greek,* 1, 134–37.

13. Brinsley, *Ludus Literarius, or the Grammar Schoole* (London, 1612), p. 41.

14. *Cato: Concerning the Precepts of Common Life* (London, 1612). *Corderius' Dialogues* (London, 1614). *Tullie's Offices* (London, 1616). *Virgil's Eclogues* (London, 1633).

boy must learn through talking and reading until he becomes almost as familiar with Latin as he is with English.[15]

Locke thus went beyond the earlier reformers, who had urged only that boys understand the reasons behind the applications of rules, not that the rules be ignored altogether. In this matter New England's schoolmasters followed the sixteenth-century reformers rather than Locke. Still, the impact of Locke's educational views was felt in New England—though largely indirectly.[16]

Few masters seem to have read his *Thoughts Concerning Education*, and of those who did fewer still threw out their grammar books and revamped their methods along the lines he prescribed. But after 1725 more and more of them used the texts of Locke's disciple, John Clarke, who in the best sensationalist manner subjected his master's suggestions to the test of the classroom and then modified them in light of the results. After teaching for a time in the grammar school in Hull, England, Clarke endorsed Locke's strictures against the traditional means of instruction, which Locke had branded the "Vulgar Method." Since Clarke's own experience had taught him that some grammar was necessary in learning Latin, he urged that boys begin reading only after they had learned the rules of declining nouns and conjugating verbs. In other ways he followed Locke—as, for example, in discounting the need for memorization.[17]

Clarke also advocated the use of Latin texts with literal English translations, and in fact published many of his own. His books offered translations that were literal in all respects but one: their Latin syntax had been altered to resemble the English

15. Locke, *Some Thought Concerning Education* (4th ed. London, 1699), pp. 294, 271–313.

16. There is no good statement of New England methods. I have extracted them from copybooks, diaries, and letters.

17. Clarke, *An Essay upon the Education of Youth in Grammar-Schools* (London, 1720), pp. 45–53.

as closely as possible—a concession forced by the doctrine that
scholars learned easiest what they understood.[18]

Smoothing the road for many boys, Clarke's texts were much
more widely adopted than were his ideas on the teaching of
Latin. In teaching, colonial masters were eclectics: old and new
methods rubbed shoulders indiscriminately in their classrooms.
Where Clarke urged only limited memorization of the rules of
grammar, they required their charges to learn whole books by
heart. He admired Latin composition; they demanded few
themes. Theory could spell out methods, but colonial practice
preferred old and familiar ways.[19]

Unaware of theory and probably also unaware that there was
anything in teaching worthy of the designation "method," the
beginner in Latin took up his accidence and discovered that
he was expected to learn it by heart. There was no nonsense
about the most popular one in New England, Ezekiel Cheever's
A Short Introduction to the Latin Tongue . . .[20] In it the student encountered what has remained mysterious to boys ever
since: rules explaining how a noun was to be declined, a verb
conjugated, and so on through elementary grammar. The ex-
planations in English—Cheever's medieval predecessors would
have scorned the book for this indulgence—are spare. "A noun
Substantive," runs one explanation with characteristic terse-
ness, "needs no other Word to show its Signification, as *Homo*,
a Man." [21] To help himself remember such nuggets the scholar
filled a small copybook with rules and illustrative examples.
Some surviving books contain what were obviously practice
exercises—adjectives, for example, declined over and over again
to impress the memory.[22]

18. Clarke translated the following authors: Suetonius, Sallust, Eutropius, Nepos,
Florus, Justin, and Ovid.

19. Clarke, pp. 16–18.

20. First published in Boston in 1709 and reprinted frequently. Cheever's authorship
has been challenged many times amid much argument. Since no matter how severe the
challenge the book has always been associated with Cheever, I have attributed it to him.

21. Cheever (Boston, 1771), p. 7.

22. Jonathan Judd Copybook, Forbes Library. Solomon Drowne Latin Exercise and
Rule Book, Drowne Papers, Brown University Library.

After mastering the accidence, or perhaps while going at it, the boy turned to a nomenclature, a book of words and sentences designed to improve the vocabulary. The most commonly used was Francis Gregory's *Nomenclature Brevis Anglo-Latino* . . . , a small volume containing columns of Latin-English words and phrases.[23] Another almost as widely known early in the century was *Orbis Sensualium Pictus* by Johann Comenius,[24] which boasted pictures with accompanying descriptions. The boy looked at the pictures, then at the text for the names of the objects he was to identify. The edition used in New England gave both Latin and English words. Had it not, the students would have been thoroughly confused, for the pictures were inexpertly drawn—flies, for example, look like bees. The English words gave a start in what must have been a puzzling job of identification.

A slightly more difficult book, Leonhard Culmann's *Sententiae Pueriles*,[25] might be substituted in place of the vocabularies. Its sentences, starting with a group of two words, were memorized and read aloud, as were those in Comenius, in order to increase vocabularies and facility in speaking Latin. Many of the sentences urge a morality every society seeks to inculcate in its young: "Exerce probitatem (exercise honesty), "Libenter disce" (learn willingly), "Legibus pare" (obey the laws); and

23. London, 1675. A copy published in Boston (1752) is in MHS inscribed "Wm Skinner Junr His Book April 2 1754"; his name also appears with the date 1761. This was probably William Skinner, son of William Skinner (A.B., Harvard, 1731). Young Skinner was ten years old in 1754. For his father see Shipton, *Biographical Sketches*, 9, 98–99. There are other copies showing student ownership at the AAS and at the Boston Public Library.

24. Many editions. I have used one edited by Charles Hoole (London, 1677), many times reprinted.

25. Culmann, *Sententiae Pueriles Anglo-Latinae pro Primus Latinae Linguae Tryonibus, ex Diversis Scriptoribus Collectae. Sentences for Children, English and Latin, for the First Entrers into Latin*, trans. Charles Hoole (Boston, 1702), was used at the Boston Latin School in 1712. See the account of the curriculum there by Master Nathaniel Williams in Kenneth B. Murdock, "The Teaching of Latin and Greek at the Boston Latin School in 1712," Col. Soc. of Mass., *Transactions*, 27 (Boston, 1932), 21–29. Copies owned by William Williams (A.B., Harvard, 1751) and Timothy Paine (A.B., Harvard, 1748) when they were grammar scholars are in the Harvard College Library.

a few have a surprisingly modern ring: "Nemini adverseris" (be against nobody), and "Omnibus placeto" (please everybody).[26]

The longer sentences probably occupied most of the scholar's time and gave him the most misery, for they and the dialogues in Mathurius Corderius' *Colloquies,*[27] a book with Latin and English columns like *Sententiae Pueriles,* provided the first real test of the grammar imbibed from Cheever's *Accidence.* Once in Corderius and in *Sententiae Pueriles,* the boy construed and parsed. Both exercises seem to have been done orally—at least, little resembling them appears in those copybooks that have come down to us.[28]

With Corderius well begun, the classics were introduced— usually Cicero's *Epistles* or his *Orations,* then perhaps Virgil's *Aeneid,* and others admired by the master. Here again, the common editions read in the schools offered a page in Latin with its English equivalent across from it. If the master favored an edition in which only the Latin text appeared, he permitted the use of a dictionary—out of fairness and, one suspects, to avoid being pestered with questions about unfamiliar words.[29]

26. Culmann, *Sententiae Pueriles,* p. 2.

27. Corderius, *Colloquia Scholastica, Anglo-Latina . . . ,* ed. and trans. Charles Hoole (London, 1657), was a version widely used until *Corderii Colloquiorum Centuria Selecta: Or a Select Century of the Colloquies of Corderius with an English Translation, as Literal as Possible,* trans. John Clarke (London, 1718) appeared. It was probably Hoole's that John Taylor used at the Boston Latin School in 1713; see Benjamin Wadsworth, Account Book, MHS. Solomon Drowne, who studied with a private master in Providence, R.I., also read Corderius, probably Clarke's edition: Solomon Drowne Diary, May 29, 1769, Drowne Papers. There are copies of Clarke's version (various editions) bearing student signatures at the AAS, Boston Public Library, and Harvard College Library.

28. The Reverend John Ballantine of Westfield, Mass., listened to one of his scholars, Nathaniel Pynchon, construe eight orations of Cicero three times. Pynchon also parsed. Journal of John Ballantine, July 20, 1759, AAS. Benjamin Wadsworth recorded the purchase of a "Construing Book," Nov. 24, 1707, for Amos Hallam: Benjamin Wadsworth Account Book, MHS.

29. For authors and works studied I have relied upon the following, among others: Journal of John Ballantine, July 20, 1759; Ezekiel Williams to John Williams, Apr. 3, 1781, MSS in CHS; Ebenezer Baldwin to Solomon Porter, Sept. 13, 1776, Baldwin Family Papers, Yale; Ebenezer Parkman Diary, Jan. 18, 1774, MHS. Dictionaries used

But the student did not simply read the classics; one day he translated aloud, the next he wrote out his translation, and on the third day he turned his own English version back into Latin in a different tense. He continued all the while to construe and parse and endeavored to fix the many rules of grammar firmly in mind. [30]

About this time he began to write Latin prose, to "make Latin." [31] Here again, manuals and phrase books came to his aid. There were a number of these; early in the century J. Garretson's *English Exercises . . . to Translate into Latin* [32] served until it was superseded by John Clarke's *An Introduction to the Making of Latin . . .*[33] In Clarke's book the familiar double columns of English and Latin were present to increase speed and prevent inaccuracies.

Greek presented fresh difficulties: an unknown alphabet, a different syntax, and different rules of grammar. But fortunately, or so thought the average boy and his fellows, masters required much less work in Greek than in Latin, and the process of learning a language was by now familiar. First the student mastered a grammar, perhaps William Camden's *Institutio*

---

are difficult to identify: in 1734 Elisha Coles, *A Dictionary, English-Latin and Latin-English* (probably London, 1677), was used in the Dorchester Grammar School; see *Boston News-Letter*, Jan. 17, 1734. In 1782 Ezekiel Williams at Nathan Tisdale's school in Lebanon asked for John Entick, *Entick's English-Latin Dictionary* (London, 1771): Ezekiel Williams, Sr., to John Williams, Nov. 8, 1782, CHS.

30. See, for example, Journal of John Ballantine, passim.

31. Copybooks give little evidence of the quality of Latin composed by boys. I have not seen a long theme.

32. 13th ed. London, 1712. [Nathan] Bailey revised this work and called his version *English and Latin Exercises for School-Boys to Translate into Latin Syntactically . . .* (5th ed. London, 1720). There is a copy at the AAS inscribed "Nathaniel Hubbard his book 1726." Hubbard attended the Cambridge Latin School in 1726: Shipton, 9, 168–69. Joseph Warren's copy is in the MHS (Warren, A.B., Harvard, 1759). There is a second copy at the AAS inscribed "Samuel Hills Book 1746" (probably A.B., Harvard, 1750).

33. 17th ed. London, 1757. Two masters who seem to have used it were Solomon Porter of East Windsor, Conn., in 1781 and John Ballantine in 1759: Solomon Porter to Simeon Baldwin, Feb. 5, 1781, Baldwin Family Papers; Journal of John Ballantine, July 20, 1759.

Graecae Grammatices Compendiaria . . . ;[34] then he took up
the Greek Testament, Isocrates, Homer, and sometimes one or
two others, construing and parsing all the while. In translating,
his master might require, as did John Ballantine of Westfield,
Massachusetts, that he turn Greek into Latin as well as into
English.[35]

So it went. Learning the rules, reciting them, parsing and
construing, translating from Latin to English and back again,
"making Latin," translating Greek, and puzzling over its rules
—this was the course the scholar followed until his master declared him ready for college.

Probably no boy learned Latin and Greek in precisely the
way sketched here, though this composite resembles closely the
experiences of many in the eighteenth century. Some masters
used slightly different methods and some preferred other books.
The differences can be illustrated by examining two courses actually followed, one early in the century and the other just before the American Revolution.

Around 1712 at the Boston Latin School boys spent their
first three years with Master Nathaniel Williams memorizing
Cheever's *Accidence* and a nomenclature, besides construing
and parsing *Sententiae Pueriles*, Cato's *Disticha*,[36] Corderius,
and Aesop's *Fables*.[37] In the fourth year they began Erasmus
with the help of a dictionary and an accidence but not an Eng-

34. London, 1629. Thomas Prince's copy with his name and the date "1701" is in
the Boston Public Library. One of the most popular lexicons used was Cornelius
Schrevelius, *Lexicon Manuale Graeco-Latinum, et Latino-Graecum* (London, 1663).
There is a copy in the Boston Public Library inscribed "Joseph Sewall His Book May 25
1703" (Sewall, A.B., Harvard, 1707). A copy of Joseph Hill's edition, *Lexicon
Manuale, Graeco-Latinum, et Latino-Graecum Primo Concinnatum . . . Cornelio
Schrevelico* (London, 1685), Yale, bears, among others, the name of Joseph Marsh
and the dates "1704" and "1706." In the latter year Marsh was master in the school
in Hingham, Mass.

35. Journal of John Ballantine, July 20, 1759.

36. Charles Hoole, *Catonis Disticha de Moribus* (London, 1619). Benjamin Wadsworth bought a "Cato" Apr. 19, 1707, for a scholar who lived with him in Boston:
Benjamin Wadsworth, Account Book.

37. Charles Hoole, *Aesop's Fables, English and Latin . . .* (London, 1567).

lish translation. They also parsed according to the rules in William Lily's *Grammar*, began Ovid's *De tristibus*, and wrote Latin from Garretson's *Exercises*.[38] The next year they added Cicero's *Epistles* and Ovid's *Metamorphoses* to their lists, continuing the while *De tristibus* and Erasmus, and Garretson's *Exercises*. They also learned rules of prosody, scanned some of the verse they read, and then, awkwardly one may suppose, turned to making their own verses. In the sixth year they encountered their first historian, Lucius Florus, as well as Cicero's *De officiis* and Virgil.[39] Style now became important: students noted the figures used in these works and attempted to incorporate them in the dialogues they wrote on Fridays. Late in the year they tried their hands at writing letters in Latin once a week. And, as if this were not enough for any boy, they began Greek and rhetoric. Their seventh and last year was similarly crowded: they read in Latin Cicero's *Orations*, Homer, and Hesiod.[40] Using Thomas Godwin's *Romance Historiae Anthologia*,[41] each boy translated a dialogue on Mondays and Tuesdays, on Wednesdays the same but from Horace; the mornings of recitation days, Thursdays and Fridays, they wrote dialogues from William Walker's *Treatise of English Particles . . .* ,[42] and in the afternoon turned a psalm or "something Divine" into Latin verse. They also wrote themes every two weeks and near the end of the year turned them into declamations.[43]

Presumably this schedule remained in force at least until 1722, the end of Nathaniel Williams's tenure. Williams, who devised it, probably drew heavily upon the methods of Ezekiel Cheever, his popular predecessor.[44] A list compiled in 1752 by student Benjamin Dolbeare, Jr., shows that by that time different books were being used. Dolbeare's list does not mention

---

38. Lily, A *Shorte Introduction of Grammar* . . . (London, 1567).
39. Probably the *Aeneid*.
40. There were several editions of these works.
41. London, 1696.
42. London, 1673.
43. Murdock, "Teaching of Latin," 27, 23, 25.
44. Ibid.

Cicero's *De officiis,* Ovid's *De tristibus,* Hesiod, Cato, *Senten-*
tiae Pueriles, Godwin, Lucius Florus, Walker, and Isocrates, but
adds Eutropius, Caesar's *Commentaries,* Clarke's *Introduction,*
Sebastian Chateillon, William King's *Heathen Gods,* and Paul
Aler's *Gradus ad Parnassum.*[45] Later lists indicate that few
changes were made until after 1783.[46]

Outside of Boston's two public grammar schools, few boys
read so many books or wrote dialogues and verses. In some
ways the course followed by Solomon Drowne of Providence in
1769–70 was more representative. At sixteen Drowne was older
than most boys when he began to study, on May 17, 1769, with
Charles Thompson, a private master and one of the first graduates of the newly founded Rhode Island College.[47] What
Drowne did for the first few days is not revealed in his diary.
He must have learned some grammar, for on May 29 he construed and parsed in Corderius; less than a month later, on June
21, he began Erasmus and seven weeks later, Justin. Erasmus
and Justin and probably Corderius occupied him until November 13, when he began Ovid. A week later he was making
Latin for the first time, using Clarke's *Introduction* and doing
his writing in a copybook he called his "Version Book." Although his first compositions were not demanding—he simply
put the proper endings on a series of verbs listed in Clarke:
"Caeno" (I do sup), "vocas" (you do call), "pugnat" (he does

45. The Dolbeare list in manuscript was at the MHS; it has been lost. There is a
facsimile in Pauline Holmes, *A Tercentenary History of the Boston Public Latin School,*
1635–1935 (Cambridge, Mass., 1935), p. 263. Chateillon, *Dialogorum Sacrorum . . .*
Libri (London, 1750 and earlier editions), 4, was a popular text. It was used in the
Dorchester Grammar School in 1734; see *Boston News-Letter,* Jan. 1734. David Ely
(A.B., Yale, 1769) owned a copy (now in Yale) in 1759, which he presumably
studied under his brother, the Rev. Richard Ely of Lyme, Conn. There are other
copies owned by grammar scholars in the Harvard College Library. See also Benjamin
Wadsworth, Account Book, passim. Full citations of the two other texts mentioned
in Dolbeare's list are King, *An Historical Account of the Heathen Gods and Heroes*
(London, 1710), and Aler, *Gradus ad Parnassum* (London, 1694, 1709).

46. Murdock, 27, 27–28.

47. *Historical Catalogue of Brown University, 1764–1914* (Providence, 1914),
p. 53.

fight)—soon he was writing complete sentences. Only his compositions for the next three weeks survived; in that period he covered six chapters in Clarke that dealt with the agreement of subject and verb, adjective and noun, transitive verbs, relative pronouns, and various special cases. Though none of these chapters was difficult, his heart was not always in his work. His sigh of relief as he finished putting into Latin one of the lofty periods dear to his time ("Learning makes Life sweet, and produces Pleasure, Tranquility, Glory and Praise") still sounds in his Version Book: "the End of the Third Chapter and am I glad of that." [48]

On December 11, three weeks after he first made Latin, Drowne began studying Greek grammar. This, Ovid, and perhaps his Latin compositions kept him busy until February 22, 1770, when he started reading the first volume of Joseph Davidson's *Works of Virgil*. On May 15, 1770, he began Cicero's *Orations* and, two days later, the second volume of Virgil.[49] He now had a full head of steam up—his college entrance examinations were only about six weeks hence. Since December he had worked his way through the Greek grammar once and on May 17, while waiting with his classmates for Greek Testaments to arrive, he began to go through it for a second time.[50] With the Greek Testament and a lexicon in hand on May 21, he construed and parsed—probably his first attempt in Greek. His diary is silent after this date until he passed his examinations for college on June 30.

Like the work of most boys in the languages, Drowne concentrated on grammar. The languages as literature remained largely a mystery to him and his fellows and, one suspects, to

48. Drowne's Diary is actually several loose pages, some very small fragments, and what he called "His Day Book." I have also used his Latin "Version Book" and a second Latin and arithmetic copybook, Drowne Papers.

49. Davidson, *The Works of Virgil Translated into English Prose* . . . (4th ed. 2 vols. London, 1763). His Diary simply mentions his beginning the first volume of Virgil—"Bought the Sett of Mr. West." There is a receipt given by Benjamin West to Drowne for 17s. 6d., "To 1 set Davidson's Virgil," in Drowne Papers.

50. Diary, Drowne Papers.

their masters. For "making Latin" with the hope of cultivating a classical style was a form without substance. Putting the proper endings on Latin words listed in a manual in order to write sentences also found in the manual improved no one's style, though it constituted a useful grammatical exercise. A knowledge of grammar hardly hurts a literary style, of course; but unaccompanied by an opportunity to compose without encumbering guides it will produce neither a classical nor any other kind of style. What Drowne learned was not how to write Latin with distinction, but how to read the language with accuracy. This and the familiarity with the classics conferred value upon the studies he undertook.

Rhetoric, defined by a Harvard Commencement thesis in 1693 as "the art of speaking and writing with elegance," [51] only occasionally appeared in the classical curriculum. Most boys probably did not study rhetoric until they reached college; even in the Boston Latin School they waited until their sixth year to begin it. Boston's boys did learn to pick out the "Elegancies" in the works they read early in their careers, a practice which may have occupied scholars in other schools as well.[52]

Both Aristotelian and Ramist texts used in the schools survive, though evidence is slim as to which was preferred, if indeed one ranked above the other. Puritan Harvard had read both, but she had prized Ramus more highly, for Ramist rhetoric appealed in its simplicity and tidiness. Aristotelian rhetoric, on the other hand, was a maze of divisions and subheadings twisting around the rubrics denoting invention, disposition, memory, elocution, and pronunciation. In the Aristotelian scheme, invention offers methods for discovering content; disposition covers form and concentrates especially on the parts of an oration; memory includes rules for memorizing a speech; elocution or style de-

51. Samuel E. Morison, *Harvard College in the Seventeenth Century* (Cambridge, Mass., 1936), p. 172.

52. Col. Soc. of Mass., *Publications*, 27, 24.

scribed literary figures; and pronunciation makes suggestions on delivery.[53]

Ramus pruned off the first three of these parts along with the labyrinth of divisions subsumed by each and thereby made rhetoric a simpler and more congenial art. More important, his excision removed the threat Puritans perceived in the Aristotelian version; the inclusion of invention and disposition made rhetoric a self-contained art capable of determining its own ends without reference to the ends of God. Thus the appeal of the Ramist redaction: it separated form from content, leaving substance to logic and theology—safer and more responsible arts. Relegated to secondary importance, rhetoric became the art of embellishment. Dialectic shaped the body, rhetoric in a subsequent act furnished only its bright clothing.[54]

This conception of rhetoric as adornment prevailed in the grammar school curriculum. At the same time schools adopted textbooks which returned invention and disposition to rhetoric. John Holmes' *The Art of Rhetoric*,[55] a textbook used in the 1760s in Rhode Island and Connecticut, first catalogues the component parts of rhetoric in good Aristotelian terms (omitting only "memory") and then in an exhibition of indiscriminate eclecticism illustrates its ideals of eloquence from both camps, citing Aristotle, Vossius, and Farnaby without embarrassment along with Ramus and Dugard.[56]

But Holmes' book is Ramist in its consideration of rhetoric as a forensic art. Rhetoric indeed seems to have become almost synonymous with oratory by the time of the Revolution. As rhetoric became more and more a verbal art, we may suppose that it lost its connection with Latin, for most scholars were probably unable to speak the language fluently. For example,

53. Miller, *New England Mind*, pp. 300–30.
54. Ibid., pp. 318–21.
55. Third impression, London, 1766.
56. James Manning, teaching in Warren, R.I., imported Holmes' *Rhetoric* and other books for his school in 1767. He offered them for sale in *Newport Mercury*, Aug. 3, 1767.

Master Charles Thompson's scholars in Providence around 1770 declaimed in English. Their description of their reasons for practicing oratory illustrates how complete the separation was: "pronounceing is of pecular Advantage to youth, both, as to pronouncing the English Tongue with proper Emphasis, and Cadence. And for the bringing up of youth with courage, that they may speak undauntedly & with propriet[y] in an Assembly of Men." [57]

Less widely taught than rhetoric, logic too was usually given in English. Like rhetoric it appeared early in the century in both Aristotelian and Ramist forms. The difference between the two was striking: Aristotelian logic emphasized the categories and the syllogism while Ramist logic discarded the categories and relegated the syllogism to a peripheral place in method. For the categories it substituted "arguments"—any words or concepts used in thinking—and for Aristotelian method, an elaborate system of classification built around dichotomies. According to Ramus, the work of logic is to divide the arguments until basic terms are reached. [58]

Neither Aristotle nor Ramus was read in New England colleges and schools, which preferred textbooks relaying diluted versions. Though little is known about what books masters employed, evidence suggests that in the eighteenth century they cared little about the old disputes between the followers of Aristotle and Ramus and used whatever was available. Daniel Brewer, Jr., for example, while at Cambridge Latin, studied the *Syntagma Logicum Aristotelico Ramaeum* of Amandi Polarii, a text which tries to find middle ground between Aristotle and Ramus by adopting ideas from both. [59]

57. Undated petition "To the Proprietors of the grammar School at Providence" (endorsed on the back of Charles Thompson's students), Drowne Papers. The date I have given is accurate, I believe, because Thompson went to Warren sometime in 1770. See *Historical Catalogue of Brown*, p. 53.

58. Miller, pp. 123–27.

59. Basel, 1611. His copy is in the Yale University Library inscribed with his name and the date Sept. 30, 1722. For Brewer see Shipton, *8*, 116.

In 1719 a text appeared which gradually earned so much respect that by the Revolution it had almost completely replaced older books. This was *Logic: or, The Right Use of Reason* by Isaac Watts,[60] a prolific English hymn and textbook writer. Watts credited neither Aristotle nor Ramus with the inspiration for his text, claiming instead that it was thoroughly Lockean. Filled with piety and common sense masquerading as logical method, Watts' text presented a simple means of arriving at the old and comforting Protestant conclusions.

Its value as a guide to logic rested on its section on syllogisms. Here despite his denial, Watts was in debt to Aristotle, for his treatment followed the system employed by logicians for centuries. In New England, at least, Watts' book was well suited to its subject; and logic like rhetoric remained mortgaged to tradition.

60. 4th ed. London, 1731. Among its earliest users may have been Hopkins Grammar School, New Haven. Moses Mansfield, rector of the school in the early 1730s, owned one.

6. The Curriculum: Arithmetic, Mathematics, Navigation, Surveying, Geography, and Astronomy

SURFEITED by the languages, Latin scholars only rarely sampled anything beyond simple arithmetic. Until the middle of the century a boy could enter either Harvard or Yale wholly ignorant of even addition and subtraction. After 1745 Yale demanded that candidates for admission know the rules of common arithmetic; Rhode Island College probably followed Yale's example, but Harvard did not require even that minimum knowledge until after the Revolution. The lack of college requirements evidently affected arithmetical study among pre-college boys. "As late as 1725," Samuel Eliot Morison reports, seniors at Harvard "had to spend a month studying Arithmetic in order to qualify for Euclid." At the other extreme stood an exceptional few who studied fluxions. Many other boys, among them a large number not destined for college, took up algebra, geometry, and trigonometry.[1]

Like Latin and Greek, arithmetic was learned from textbooks, though often teachers dictated problems which boys copied and solved. Almost all the textbooks were written and published in England. Cocker's and Hodder's texts, both used in the seventeenth century, dominated the market until early in the eight-

---

1. For Harvard see "Harvard College Records," Col. Soc. of Mass., *Publications*, 31, 329; 15, 134; *Massachusetts Gazette and Boston Weekly News-Letter*, Oct. 17, 1771. For Yale, Dexter, *Biographical Sketches of the Graduates of Yale*, 1, 347; 2, 2 (for the 1745 requirement). The Morison statement is in *Harvard in the Seventeenth Century*, p. 208.

eenth century, when others, especially those by John Hill, John Ward, and Thomas Dilworth, cut into their field.[2] These books are strikingly alike. All cover about the same topics from addition through geometric progression, and all explain their subject in about the same way. Under each topic a general definition is first given—"A Fraction is that which represents . . ."—followed by an explanation of lesser terms—"the denominator is . . ."[3] After the opening treatment a series of problems illustrating the concepts explained is presented. The solution of problems in turn follows a careful sequence: first, the rule applying a general case is stated, then a problem is given, and finally the solution, usually with all elements of the computation, is worked out.[4]

Several textbooks include instruction in higher mathematics as well as in arithmetic. Hill's *Arithmetick* offers a few simple algebra problems, and Ward's *The Young Mathematician's Guide* provides substantial material on algebra, geometry, conic sections, and the "Arithmetic of Infinites."

For a more thoroughgoing treatment of higher mathematics scholars turned to larger works, among them Nathaniel Hammond, *The Elements of Algebra in a New and Easy Method;*[5] Benjamin Martin, *The Young Trigonometer's Compleat Guide;*[6] W. Emerson, *A Treatise of Algebra;*[7] Joseph Fenn, *A New and Complete System of Algebra;*[8] and one of several editions of

2. Edward Cocker, *Cocker's Arithmetick* (London, 1688, many editions). James Hodder, *Hodder's Arithmetick or, That Necessary Art Made Most Easie* (15th ed. London, 1685). John Hill, *Arithmetick, both in Theory and Practice, Made Plain and Easy in All the Common and Useful Rules, both in Whole Numbers and Fractions, Vulgar and Decimal* (London, 1745). John Ward, *The Young Mathematician's Guide. Being a Compendium of Arithmetic, Both Practical and Theoretical* (12th ed. London, 1764). There are copies of all these books, bearing marks of student use, in Yale. I have seen others in AAS, MHS, Harvard College Library, and Boston Public Library.

3. See especially texts by Hodder, Cocker, Hill, and Dilworth.

4. Ibid.

5. London, 1742. There is one in Yale with Samuel Darling's name in it. Darling (A.B. Yale, 1769) was rector of Hopkins Grammar School in New Haven 1770–71.

6. London, 1736.

7. London, 1764.

8. Dublin, 17—?.

Euclid.[9] Just as in arithmetic these books concentrate on problems, but they too give attention to the "rules." And in higher mathematics, as in arithmetic, masters seem to have followed the familiar road in teaching: first the rules were to be learned and then the problems solved. Master Samuel Lloyd of New Haven promised that in geometry and trigonometry "the Theory of each will be clearly laid down in a few plain Rules." [10] The test of a scholar's knowledge, however, was not in repeating rules but in solving problems.

Geometry, of course, involved some drawing. Master Job Palmer's manuscript text contains many problems dealing with such subjects as bisecting lines and angles, dropping perpendiculars, and constructing triangles. Palmer's protractor looks to be the product of his own devising, made on heavy paper with lines, divisions, and numbers carefully inked in. No doubt other masters instructed their scholars in how to make protractors, for even such simple instruments were hard to come by.[11]

Obviously the immediate end of studying mathematics was to learn to add and subtract and to perform more complicated tasks. If textbooks and copybooks reveal something about the content and methods of instruction and hint at their quality, they also exhibit an area in which curriculum responded to the most pressing needs of the culture sustaining the schools. They show that in New England where men with skills necessary to a commercial society were required, mathematics was bent to the practical. John Hill's textbook, for example, explains how to compute simple and compound interest, profit and loss on simple transactions, stock dividends ("the Rule of Fellowship"), besides giving problems in "barter and alligation," as methods of

9. John Keil, *Euclids Elements of Geometry* (London, 1723).

10. *Connecticut Journal & New Haven Post-Boy*, Apr. 30, 1773.

11. MSS text and protractor are in Yale. For Palmer, master of Roxbury Grammar, see Shipton, *Biographical Sketches*, 10, 393. There are many similar copybooks in the Uncatalogued MSS of the Essex Institute; one inscribed with the names of Benjamin Boardman, John Hall, and John Devotion in Yale; and one, Solomon Nash's Copybook, in New Haven Colony Historical Society.

mixing different quantities were called. Most of the other texts also present these topics, and several include instruction in annuities, reversions, dialing, and gauging. Can we be sure that these subjects were taught? Copybooks and newspaper advertisements reveal that they were.[12] Even boys like John and Obadiah Brown of Providence, who must have been steeped in commercial practices while preparing to take their places in the family countinghouse, received an early introduction to business while learning simple arithmetic in school.[13]

For more thorough business training, of course, a boy could resort to a master who taught bookkeeping. Knowledge of simple arithmetic was all that was required for its study—though patience must have been almost as necessary, for there were a large number of ledgers and "books" to learn.[14] Only one form of bookkeeping seems to have been taught—double entry; and only one version was respectable—the "Italian Form." Probably few masters required textbooks in their teaching, but those who did seem to have favored John Mair's manuals.[15]

Bookkeeping required boys to learn to keep ledgers; but in almost every other kind of mathematical study they wrote in copybooks, small notebooks with their pages stitched together. The meticulous boy divided his into sections and chapters, each headed by an appropriate rubric such as "addition" or "subtraction." Problems filled most pages. Some masters imposed the dreary labor of adding columns of figures or the conversion of units of money into units of a different value. But there were bright spots, such as the problem found in the copybook kept by Solomon Drowne: "The Circumference of the Earth, as well as all other Circles are Divided into 360 Degrees and each De-

12. See the Uncatalogued MSS, Essex Institute; and Copybooks in New Haven Colony Historical Society, in RIHS and Yale.

13. Cipher Book of John Brown, and Obadiah Brown Ciphering Book: both in RIHS.

14. Bookkeeping guides commonly listed, among others, cash book, invoice book, sales book, receipt book, and waste-book.

15. John Mair, *Book-keeping Methodize'd: or, A Methodical Treatise of Merchant-Accompts, According to the Italian Form* (Edinburgh, 1773).

gree into 60 Miles, Now I Demand how many Miles Furlongs Poles yards Feet and Barley corns will reach round the Globe of the Earth?" [16] (Figuring three barley corns to an inch, Drowne had no trouble solving the problem.) And there were also the copybook's margins. They were the private domain of the boy, where he might write out multiplication tables, solve problems of his own devising, or merely trace the names of himself or those of his friends. Young John Brown found room in his to scrawl ebulliently: "John Brown the cleverest Boy in Providence Town." [17] Dreamers of far-off places, or at least of places more interesting than the classroom, drew pictures of ships and fish. Much loving care seems to have been given to miniature portraits of the artist as fisherman landing a big one.

To landlubbers navigation always has appeared a mysterious art connected somehow with the mariner's compass and "shooting" the stars. New England boys who grew up in ports knew that there was more to it, but they often found locating a ship on the sea, or on a chart in a classroom, mysterious enough.

Some who studied navigation never handled a quadrant or a cross staff, never kept a navigator's journal, and never went to sea. Equally landlocked, their masters looked upon navigation as a branch of mathematics and taught it to strengthen the mathematical knowledge of their scholars.[18] There was, for example, the course Master Job Palmer taught at Middleborough in 1739, the year of his graduation from Harvard, and at the Roxbury Grammar School a few years later. If his large, well-kept manual of navigation can be trusted, he gave his charges little instruction in the skills a working navigator required. But his handbook contains many practical problems—finding course and distance for example—all represented graphically and all

16. Drowne Papers, Brown University Library.

17. In RIHS.

18. Master Joseph Kent of Boston, who lacked practical experience, advertised in 1737: "Navigation, or any other Branch of the Mathematicks,": *Boston Weekly News-Letter*, July 7, 1737.

solved mathematically. Graphic representations illustrated the mathematics clearly, though few of them were the kinds of drawings a seagoing navigator would be likely to have made. Palmer began with the application of right angles "to Sailing," and proceeded to plane and oblique triangles. He then explained the Mercator projection, and how it could be applied in navigation. From Mercator he moved into latitude and longitude problems which involved a ship's position when two of three elements—course, distance, and latitude—were known. After this he considered spherical triangles, and the computation of position from data obtained from observations. Like all his problems, these too are represented graphically and mathematically in his text.[19]

A lad who worked Palmer's problems carefully would comprehend the navigator's task without having the vaguest idea of how it was performed on the sea. He would not know how to make observations or how to keep a chart. He would not know how to use the common navigational instruments or how to keep a journal. Nor would he have a "feel" for the difficulties navigators commonly experienced—unexpected currents, cloudy days which hid sun and stars, and the puzzle of finding longitude. But his knowledge of geometry—and, to some extent, trigonometry—would benefit. Palmer's course, indeed, was an exciting way of learning higher mathematics.[20]

Schoolmasters who gave more practical navigation had to reckon with higher mathematics and theory, though not to the extent that instructors like Palmer did. For example, Captain George MacKay of Boston taught geometry and trigonometry along with the use of the plain scale, the Gunter, the sliding Gunter, and Sector—all instruments used by navigators.[21] A

19. Job Palmer MSS, Navigation Book, Yale. I have also relied upon a second MSS Navigation Book in Yale which belonged to Reuben Haines; dated Oct. 25, 1770. There are many MSS books kept by boys in Salem schools in the Uncatalogued MSS, Essex Institute. I have found the bundles marked "Navigation School" and "Algebra, Geometry, Trigonometry, Navigation, Surveying, Salem & Essex County" most useful.

20. The manuscript manuals mentioned in footnote 19 confirm this.

21. *Boston Weekly News-Letter*, Sept. 12, 1754.

few masters apparently ignored higher mathematics altogether. John Leach, a mariner who left the sea for the classroom after service in the Royal Navy and three voyages in the pay of the East India Company, broke his scholars in on navigational instruments, then taught them "Journal-keeping in a Practical Method," finishing their training with instruction in "Drawing, as far as is useful for a compleat Sea-Artist, as it respects taking Prospects of Land and surveying Harbours." [22]

Several textbooks struck a balance between theory and practice. J. Barrow's *Navigator's Britannica,* for example, allots several chapters to mathematics and others to the solution of position problems and the use of instruments.[23] All the texts reveal the conservatism of navigators—old techniques are explained as fully as the newer ones, and the most common navigational practices such as plain sailing and great circle sailing receive the most complete treatment.[24]

No matter how careful a master was to instruct his boys in the use of instruments, "practical" navigation could not become really practical until it deserted the schoolhouse for the sea. Surveying instruction, on the other hand, could shift from classroom to the field and back again with little trouble. This was the way some, perhaps most, masters taught it.

Since a surveyor required only arithmetic and simple geometry in his work, there was less need for textbooks than in navigation. A few mathematics texts contained some information on the subject, and they may have been used occasionally. Perhaps the most popular text was John Love's *Geodasia: or, the*

22. Ibid., Oct. 17, 1754.

23. J. Barrow, *Navigatio Britannica: or a Complete System of Navigation in All Its Branches, Both with Regard to Theory and Practice* (London, 1750).

24. Among the texts most widely used were Matthew Norwood, *Norwood's System of Navigation: Teaching the Whole Art* . . . (London, 1685); James Atkinson, *Epitome of the Art of Navigation* (London, 1765); Nathaniel Colson, *The Mariners New Kalendar* . . . (London, 1751); Henry Wilson, *Navigation New Modelled* . . . (London, 1750); and Thomas Haselden, *The Seaman's Daily Assistant* . . . (London, 1774).

Art of Surveying.[25] It furnished arithmetical guidance and a little geometry. The bulk of the book concerns practical surveying: the use of instruments, and the measure, division, and laying out of lands. Job Palmer's manuscript text,[26] which defines surveying as "the Art of Measuring, Laying out, Dividing & Levelling of Land," [27] follows about the same plan. Like most masters, Palmer refrained from describing most of the instruments of surveying until he took his scholars into the field. Instead, he described the general procedure a surveyor followed —the measuring of lines and angles, the recording of data in the "Field Book," and the plotting and compilation of data. ("The Last thing is to Cast up the Contents of a Field, in Acres, Roods, and Perches").[28]

Since a surveyor faced many problems in going about his business, Palmer next took up the "Usual" and the "curious cases in the Measuration of Land." Among others these included variously shaped fields, taking the plot of a field with a chain alone, the semicircle alone, from one station and so on. Palmer passed along what lore of the craft he knew, telling the boys, for example, that large fields were "best Surveyed" by going around their sides with the chain, ignoring their diagonals, and taking the measure of the angles with a semicircle or circumferentor.[29]

Practicing surveyors weighed their instruction even more in favor of field work than Palmer did. But in the classroom or the field, boys must have found in the subject a graphic demonstration of mathematical principles.

Boys who studied navigation required some knowledge of the earth and the heavens. Therefore masters giving navigation in-

25. 9th ed. London, 1771.

26. MSS Mathematics Book, Yale.

27. Ibid., p. 31.

28. Ibid., p. 35.

29. Ibid., pp. 38–45, passim. The semicircle and circumferentor were widely used instruments.

BELMONT UNIVERSITY LIBRARY

struction frequently also taught geography and astronomy. These subjects, also valued for themselves, often appeared in schools that did not teach navigation. Though they employed the usual classroom devices of study in texts followed by recitations, masters also put their charges to studying maps and globes. And occasionally they taught projecting the sphere.[30]

The staple of geographical provender was not, however, maps or globes, but the textbook. Such books usually linked astronomy to their subject, a conjunction that suggests that the two were sometimes studied together. But these texts always gave far more treatment to the earth than to the stars.

Most of the books—Thomas Salmon's, Patrick Gordon's, and William Guthrie's, for example—are much alike; large books with a huge assortment of accurate information but with almost an equal amount of myth and fancy.[31] Gordon's *Geography Anatomiz'd*, probably the most widely used text during the first half of the century, must have delighted boys with its wild tales, subsumed under the deceptively toneless rubric "Geographical Paradoxes." Number three challenged the reader's image-making power: "There is a certain place of the Earth, at which if two Men should chance to meet, one would stand upright upon the Soles of the others Feet, and neither of them should feel the other's Weight, and yet they both should retain their Natural Posture." [32] Number thirty-one titillated his palate: "There is a certain Country in South America, many of whose Savage Inhabitants are such unheard of Canibals, that they not only feed upon Human Flesh, but also some of them do actually eat themselves, and yet they commonly survive that

30. *Boston News-Letter*, Mar. 21, 1709; Oct. 9, 1735; Sept. 12, 1754. *Connecticut Journal and New Haven Post-Boy*, Apr. 30, 1773.

31. Thomas Salmon, *A New Geographical and Historical Grammar; Containing the True Astronomical and Geographical Knowledge of the Terraqueous Globe . . .* (12th ed. London, 1771). Patrick Gordon, *Geography Anatomiz'd: or, the Geographical Grammar* (9th ed. London, 1722). William Guthrie, *A New Geographical, Historical, and Commercial Grammar; and Present State of the Several Kingdoms of the World* (London, 1770).

32. Gordon, *Geography Anatomiz'd*, p. 36.

strange Repast." [33] All proceed on the assumption that geography is best studied along national lines. Each describes the "four" continents—Europe, Asia, Africa, and America—then turns to individual nations. (The American continent is accorded slight treatment in these books; New England is hardly discussed.) The geography of a nation is interpreted by all to include not only its physical features but also its political history, constitution, religion, institutions, manufactures, coinage, and a host of other matters. Since these subjects are not integrated into any meaningful whole, or even connected, each text takes on the appearance of an encyclopedia. Still, remembering that boys have much less use for order than their elders, one may suppose that they enjoyed and even profited from these books. So however much New England pride may have suffered from the scant attention paid the Puritan colonies, New England provincialism surely must have diminished.

These texts and an occasional manual of astronomy furnished young scholars with their first knowledge of the cosmos. For the most part they described the universe of Copernicus and Kepler, and to some extent Newton. Schoolmasters, too, doubtless taught the new astronomy, for both Harvard and Yale held that the true conception of the universe was Copernican.[34]

But vestiges of Ptolemaic astronomy appeared at odd places in the curriculum. A Latin scholar ordinarily not introduced to astronomy in his preparation for college might in his innocence drink in the Ptolemaic version as he studied the phrases in Comenius. This was as true late in the eighteenth century as it was at the century's opening. A sketch in Comenius pictures the earth lying at the center of the universe. Accompanying it is a simple statement of the Ptolemaic world view: "The Heaven is wheeled about and encompasseth the Earth standing in the middle." [35] And a geography text used early in the century takes

33. Ibid., pp. 39–40.

34. Morison, p. 216. See also Issac Watts, *The Knowledge of the Heavens and the Earth Made Easy: or, The First Principles and Geography* (London, 1726).

35. Johan Amos Comenius, *Orbis Sensualium Pictus* (London, 1672), p. 11.

no stand at all on the new astronomy, but merely states the positions of both new and old.[36]

The textbooks do not give a sophisticated version of the new astronomy. Though they describe the universe of Kepler, Copernicus, and Newton, they ignore the mathematics which made the new system intelligible. Almost all fail to mention the law of gravitation, though in their pages, as in much eighteenth-century writing, Newton reigns a virtual monarch. Despite this omission the books convey the most important point their writers wished to make: the universe has a divine purpose. During the period when the earth was thought to rest at the center of the universe, God's design had been evident. But with the discoveries of the new astronomy and the shift of center to the sun, Christians at first feared that God might be discarded. Such fears were groundless. The order, the harmony, and even the vastness of the new universe were taken as evidence of God's glory; if anything, they demonstrated that He was mightier and wiser than men had suspected.

This point made, the texts could afford to ignore mathematical description. Their authors' compulsion to draw the old moral from the new world picture had produced not only elementary manuals but a restatement of a comforting Christian belief.

36. Lawrence Eachard, *A Most Compleat Compendium of Geography* . . . (2d ed. London, 1691).

7. The Curriculum: The "Female Branches" of Learning

> Nothing so true as what you once let fall,
> "Most Women have no Characters at all."
> Matter too soft a lasting mark to bear,
> And best distinguished by black, brown, or fair.

THUS Alexander Pope ridiculed women and by so doing pleased New Englanders with his wit. For New Englanders shared the prejudice of the time that relegated women to home and hearth. A woman, the eighteenth century knew, began life with an inborn disadvantage—an intelligence weaker in power and narrower in scope than a man's. Her mind did not permit her to comprehend the arts and sciences or to participate in the world of commerce, politics, and war. This left the home as the only proper place for her. There she was to occupy herself with domestic cares, her children and her husband. Not surprisingly, unmarried women were not admired. Wits poked fun at spinsters, however knowledgeable—better an uneducated wife than an educated virgin.

Even women who supported themselves came in for a good deal of scorn. And a number of women, usually in cities and towns, did make their own livings. Some served as apprentices in order to enter such occupations as hairdressing, embroidery, and dressmaking. Others taught school, bound books, and ran print shops. Boston even supported a woman shoemaker for a time, Elizabeth Shaw, who had been trained in London.[1]

1. Lawrence C. Wroth, *The Colonial Printer* (Portland, Maine, 1938), pp. 190–91, 200. For Elizabeth Shaw see Carl Bridenbaugh, *The Colonial Craftsman* (New York, 1950), p. 106.

Impressed by this record of advance, some historians have argued that life in the colonies worked a genuine shift upward in the status of women.[2] They have failed to notice that most women remained unaffected by these changes. In any case, a large number of those who entered business or who worked in crafts were widows or married women helping their husbands. In assisting her husband, a woman engaged in an activity sanctioned by the time, for work under a husband's direction testified to his superior status. As for widows in business, this practice was not peculiar to the colonies; widows in western Europe often assumed such responsibilities.[3]

Certainly the occupational concessions women extracted from a male world did not shake colonial conviction that their education should aim at making them good wives. Becoming a good wife meant recognizing one's duties and learning how to carry them out. Though parents and ministers could be counted on to make a girl realize her obligations and to teach her much about meeting them, the school was expected to assist.

Beyond the subjects making up the curricula offered by girls' schools, little is known of how and what girls learned. They used few books and those few were mostly the books of elementary schools—primers, readers, and simple arithmetics.

They needed no text for sewing which they learned under the instruction of an experienced teacher. (Many a girl required only the supervision of her mother, who at least could teach "plain needlework.") With private teachers they entered into more complicated work—dresden, embroidery, and tent stitch among others, and then, as a last step, making clothing.

When they came to academic subjects, girls received about the same kinds of instruction as boys, but they do not seem to have pursued their studies as extensively. The arithmetic they learned illustrates this point. Girls memorized the same rules

2. See Daniel Boorstin, *The Americans: The Colonial Experience* (New York, 1958), pp. 186–87.
3. Wroth, p. 154.

that boys did, solved the same problems, and kept copybooks
with rules, problems, and computations arranged under the same
rubrics. But here they stopped; algebra, geometry, and other
branches of mathematics were not for them. Similarly, newspaper advertisements suggest that the geography imbibed by
girls was simple fare concentrating on the use of globes.[4]

The English that girls studied was more rigorous. Though its
focus was grammatical, girls wrote compositions and letters, and
read eighteenth-century poetry and prose.[5] The Reverend Ebenezer Parkman of Westborough, Massachusetts, whose daughter
Molly borrowed *Pamela* and *Clarissa Harlowe* from a neighbor,
approved of these books. They afforded, he wrote, poor country
girls unable to live in boarding schools "some Taste of brilliant
sense, when they cant be polished by Conversation." But he added
the warning that "this indulgence had need be kept under a
Strict Guard, & Caution." [6]

Female education obviously did not come up to that enjoyed
by boys. Even if a girl went off to boarding school, as did Mary
Fish of Stonington, Connecticut, she came away with very little
of intellectual value. Daughter of the Reverend Joseph Fish,
Mary was fifteen years old when in 1751 her father placed her
in Mrs. Sarah Osborn's boarding school at Newport. Up to
that time she had attended "the best schools Stonington afforded," [7] but she apparently had not learned much more
than how to read and write. Her father contributed to this
early education: every morning after family prayers he listened to her read and then gave "advice for the day." [8] He

4. To determine the level of girls' achievements in arithmetic, I have relied upon
arithmetic copybooks in the Uncatalogued MSS, Essex Institute, and scattered ones
elsewhere, e.g. Alice Chase's copybook [1755] in RIHS. For advertisements describing or mentioning geography see *The Independent Chronicle and The Universal Ad-
vertiser*, Apr. 28, 1779, Mar. 23, 1780; *Conn. Journal*, Oct. 22, 1783.

5. *Newport Mercury*, July 17, 1769. *Essex Gazette*, May 26, 1776. *Boston News-
Letter*, Apr. 28, 1774.

6. Quotations are from Shipton, *Biographical Sketches*, 6, 514.

7. Mary Dickinson, "Reminiscences," p. 4, Silliman Family Papers, Yale.

8. Ibid., p. 4.

also urged her to study her Bible and, of course, saw to it that she kept the Sabbath. Mrs. Osborn, zealous to be "instrumental in promoting the good of souls," [9] continued Mary's religious instruction and taught her fancy needlework, but not much else. Mary stayed for two months, the last period of formal schooling in her life.[10]

The subjects Mary studied furnished the chief intellectual fare for girls throughout the eighteenth century. Occasionally girls with enlightened parents, who also had the means, studied further. Genteel education in England, which served as a model for some upper class colonial parents, required that a girl know how to dance and how to sing or play a musical instrument. She should also have some knowledge of painting, have sampled geography and history, and have a passing knowledge of French. Although few colonial girls encountered all these subjects, after the middle of the century they commanded greater approval. For example, Sally Burr, Timothy Edwards' ward, seems to have studied both geography and history. Her guardian evidently wanted her challenged intellectually, for he recommended history as "one of the Best means to open, enlarge, improve the Mind, & Clear it of Narrow & vulgar Prejudices." [11] Sally also seems to have spent some time practicing her handwriting. The woman charged with her care in Boston approved of this regime, but she also offered to teach Sally "Genteel Cookery." [12]

A few girls mastered "ornamental" handwriting, which was valued as a mark of genteel education. Twelve-year-old Sally Beers of New Haven filled a notebook in 1776 and 1777 with highly embellished writing, some in bright red ink! The verses she selected to copy (or were selected for her) included some Christian exhortations, and most show how urgent was the quest for gentility. Thus the lines under the rubric "Painting":

9. Samuel Hopkins, *Memoirs of the Life of Mrs. Sarah Osborn* (Worcester, Mass., 1799), p. 61.

10. Dickinson, "Reminiscences," pp. 5–6.

11. Sarah Gill to Timothy Edwards, Oct. 1770, Park Family Papers, Yale. (Mrs. Gill repeats Edwards' instructions in this letter.)

12. Sarah Gill to Timothy Edwards, Oct. 1770, Park Family Papers.

> Long time the Sister Arts in Iron Sleep.
> A heavy Sabbath did Supinely Keep
> At length in Raphaels Age at once they rise
> Stretch all their Limbs & open all their Eyes
> Thence rose the Roman & the Lombard Line
> One Colour'd best and one did best Design
> Raphaels Like Homors was the nobler Part
> But Titians Painting Look'd like Virgils Art
>
>   .   .   .
>
> By slow Degrees the Painting Art advanc'd
> As Man grew polish'd.[13]

Sally also paid her respects to the conventional virtues so congenial to a commercial society, copying in her book in answer to the question "How to get Riches":

> The Art of growing Rich consists
> much in Thrift. All men are not
> Qualified for getting Money, but it is in the
> Power of every one alike to Practice this virtue.[14]

This represented what writers on the female branches of education liked to call "solid improvement"—a girl might study painting, but she should never lose sight of moral principles.

Combining as they did the persistent concern for morality and utility with newer aspirations toward gentility, educations like the one Sally evidently received entailed no clear break with the past. But approval of genteel education was given only grudgingly in New England. The suspicion lingered that the ornamental subjects would rob the old virtues of their power. There was doubt that a girl who read novels, danced, painted, and composed verse could be expected to maintain a home in which obedience, hard work, and religion were exalted. Moreover, genteel education enjoined concern with self ("Cultivate

13. Sally Beers Penmanship Copybook, New Haven Colony Historical Society.
14. Ibid.

your talents" was its leading imperative) while the old morality
demanded self-abnegation (a woman should serve her husband
and children first).[15]

So deeply rooted was this traditional view that repudiations
of it sometimes drew unusual arguments. Advocates of gentility
even appropriated the terminology of contemporary aesthetics
on behalf of women's education.

A cardinal feature of American aesthetic theory was its insistence that improved nature, preferably according to classical
models, was more beautiful than nature untouched by man.
Indeed, nature polished by man was one of the marks which
distinguished civilization from savagery. This attitude displayed
itself in everything from gardens to poetry.[16]

Some devotees of genteel education saw nothing incongruous
about employing the theory, proclaiming the beauty of the
polished mind just as confidently as of the clipped hedge. They
insisted that the rude female mind demanded cultivation if true
feminine beauty was to be created. Such writers idealized woman
in ways American romantics were to make familiar. Woman,
they held, was not inferior to man in all respects. Her nature
was finer, her morals purer, and her sensibilities keener. But
these characteristics disqualified her from participation in the
workaday world just as completely as the older evaluation of her
talents had. Woman was now thought to be too pure, too fine,
for coarse male activity. But then, what area of life did this leave
for her? Where should she exert herself? The answer was that
the should attempt to raise the "tone" of life; her sphere was
that "which has the heart for its object, which is secured by

15. For schools giving genteel education see *Essex Gazette,* Apr. 20, 1773, July 19,
1774; *Massachusetts Gazette and Boston Weekly News-Letter,* Apr. 1, 1773; Apr. 28,
1774.

16. I have relied on essays in the newspapers for this view. Curiously, American
aesthetic theory still held propositions discarded in eighteenth-century England. The
eighteenth-century English garden, for example, was famed for its irregular natural
beauty without symmetry and without clipped hedges or clipped trees. See B. Sprague
Allen, *Tides in English Taste (1619–1800): A Background for the Study of Literature*
(2 vols. Cambridge, Mass., 1937), I, 114–62.

meekness and modesty, by soft attractions and virtuous love." [17]
This may have been sentimentality, but it left its mark on both
educational theory and practice.[18]

Such theory prescribed that a girl's finer side be developed
through an education which resembled in some aspects the liberal
education of the eighteenth century. According to a writer in
the *New London Gazette*, history, biography, and memoirs
should be read to enable a girl to find models of virtue which
she could emulate and vices she could shun. Reading travel accounts was recommended in the belief that they would enlarge
her mind. Once equipped with knowledge of the arts, she would
serve not merely as a household drudge and not simply as a
purveyor of the old moralities, but also as a companion and
friend to her husband, capable of lighting his life with charm
and sensibility.[19]

Thus the theory ennobled woman at the same time it reaffirmed
her inferiority. And the purpose of her education remained the
same: to enable her to serve in a man's world. Still, the new
theory, by challenging tradition, held possibilities for vast improvement in her status. New conditions after the Revolution
were to make possible the realization of some of this potential.

17. *New-London Gazette*, July 13, 1770.
18. This paragraph is largely based on exchanges between "Philomathes" and
"Camilla," *New-London Gazette*, June 2, 22; July 13, 1770, and upon scattered
comments in essays in other newspapers.
19. *New-London Gazette*, July 13, 1770.

PART II

THE TRADITION ALTERED, 1784–1800

8. Educational Thought in the New Republic

THE American Revolution offers the spectacle, unfamiliar to modern eyes, of a revolution unaccompanied by social upheaval. Not that breaking the imperial bond was a tidy affair: Tories were driven out, their land seized and sold off, churches were disestablished, and primogeniture, entail, and quitrents were eliminated. But these changes effected no profound shifts in American society. Many ejected Tories soon returned, usually without making more than a perfunctory show of allegiance to the new nation; and as all classes had produced Tories, no wholesale displacement of one class by another took place even where they did not return. Nor did sale of confiscated property create a radically different distribution of wealth, for landowners seized the opportunity—which lack of money denied to the poor —to enlarge their holdings. Though disestablishment of churches was not unimportant, it did not occur everywhere; in New England, for example, the Congregational churches retained state support. And long before the Revolution, primogeniture, entail, and quitrents had lost whatever importance they had held.

If the Revolution was limited in its effects, its promoters, who remained in command throughout its course, never intended that it be anything else. One aim obsessed them: the severance of the tie to Britain. The status of persons, the class structure, the religious situation, the distribution of land, and most other arrangements affecting their society's health and stability were satisfactory. They and most of their supporters in all classes had decided upon revolution after they became convinced that the constitutional problem could be solved only by separation from Britain.

Once begun, the Revolution presented opportunities to dissatisfied groups for change. Since these groups were few and concerned only with parochial problems, no great social shifts were threatened. And American society, though encumbered with rigidities such as established churches, was flexible enough to concede that some grievances deserved satisfaction.

As they were elsewhere, the forces of internal change in New England were slender. To be sure, Massachusetts was convulsed by Shays' Rebellion, the most serious outburst anywhere of the Revolutionary era. It exposed a breach which frightened even Washington, but despite the brief savagery it provoked, Shays' was soon over, its damage repaired, its grievances partially satisfied, and its participants received back into full citizenship. For Shays' objectives were limited; its rebels did not intend to destroy the major props of society, though their assaults on the courts seemed ominous to men of substance.

While substantial men agreed that the structure of society should remain undisturbed, they conceded that marginal changes might sometimes be necessary. On the status of the Congregational Church, for example, they remained unyielding, brushing aside dissenters' demands that it be disestablished. But slavery, they agreed, was an evil; and they moved cautiously to eliminate it. They did not pass legislation emancipating slaves despite the Quakers' persistent invoking of the doctrine "created equal." Doubtless few men were unmoved by this claim; but extended to Negro slaves, it challenged the rights of property which were central not only to Revolutionary doctrine but to the social stability of New England. Obviously the institution itself could not be attacked directly; the safest course was to prohibit the slave trade, an action all the New England states took by 1790.

Though New England's chief institutions survived the Revolution almost totally unaltered, its cast of mind did not. The change was not so much in substance as in mood. Found in Americans everywhere, the new frame of mind was induced by the freedom the new nation enjoyed. Freedom made Americans self-conscious; it engaged their attention to the problem of what they were; it stretched their sense of what they might become. So preoccupied, they became eager in the search for fresh ideas about their future. As the Reverend David M'Clure rejoiced, a "spirit of enquiry" had captured Americans.[1] Especially was this true in New England, where, however, Yankees characteristically spent far more time following the lead of the inquiring spirit than delighting in it.[2]

For New Englanders were active men. Above all, they wanted with other Americans to build a unique nation, immune to the corruptions which had befallen Europe. So insistent were they that their new nation differ from European states that their descriptions of it became almost stylized: in America the arts would be made to yield finer fruits than anywhere else, nature would at last be forced to divulge her innermost secrets, institutions would reach a new purity, and in fact progress in all areas of life would await only effort. This conception prompted Noah Webster to call for an America "as independent and illustrious in letters as she is already in arms and civil policy" and in his *Grammatical Institute* to reject English usage in favor of American.[3]

Sustaining New Englanders' desires was the assurance that the

1. David M'Clure, *An Oration on the Advantages of an Early Education . . .* (Exeter, N.H., 1783), p. 15.

2. For the new mood of Americans in the early Republic see almost any newspaper or magazine published in New England, especially *Massachusetts Magazine*, *Massachusetts Centinel* (later the *Columbian Centinel*), *Providence Gazette*, *Newport Mercury*, *New Haven Gazette and Connecticut Magazine* (Meigs and Dana, printers), *New Haven Gazette* (Abel Morse printer).

3. The quotation is from Harry R. Warfel, ed., *Letters of Noah Webster* (New York, 1953), p. 6. For views of America like the one described here which reveal cultural nationalism see *Newport Mercury*, Aug. 7, 1784; *Rural Magazine or Vermont Repository*, 1, 5–13 (Jan. 1795); *New Haven Gazette and Connecticut Magazine*, June 22, 1786, Feb. 1, 1787, May 3, 1787; Jedidiah Morse, *The American Geography, or A View of the Present Situation of the United States of America* (London, 1792), preface.

Creator smiled upon their nation, that indeed their dream was
resonant with American destiny. The Lord, they believed, intended that America should reach a grand plane; he had in fact
chosen their nation to fulfill a cosmic design. The signs of the
Lord's favor, they now perceived, were manifest. The size of the
American wilderness with its tremendous forests, lakes, and
mountains which once seemed so terrifying now reassured them
by its very immensity. In such surroundings American genius
could prove itself the superior of any in the world. This faith
led men to prophesy that in America

> virtuous freedom crowned with the laurels of victory ever
> opposing ambition, will cherish future geniuses that will
> arise, to eclipse the glory of former ages! The prodigious
> continent, extending thro' various climates and regions,
> luxuriant in soil, will crown the arts and sciences with the
> productions of her worthy sons. Empire having reached
> the limits of the globe, will probably here rest, after its
> long travel from the eastern hemisphere, and the arts and
> sciences attain their last polish of perfection.[4]

In their vision of the American fate, New Englanders assigned
particular significance to the political experiment the new nation
was undertaking. This was natural; with other Americans they
had recently thrust monarchy from their shores, and the effort
had left them intensely conscious of political arrangements.
Monarchy, of course, they despised. Once rid of it they did not
have to grope for a suitable form to replace it—they became at
once ardent republicans.

Their conception of a republic was simple and clear-cut. Unlike a monarchy where power emanated from one man, a republic
drew its strength from the people to whom ultimately all political authority belonged. Through the state, elected representatives
exercised this root authority. But the ends of power were not

---

4. M'Clure, *Oration*, p. 16. For similar expressions of faith in American destiny see
New Haven Gazette and Connecticut Magazine, Feb. 16, Apr. 27, 1786; Jan. 25, 1787;
Gentlemen and Ladies Town and Country Magazine, Feb. and May 1789.

for them to determine, had in fact been prefigured in the republican ideal which promised that power was to be exercised for public purposes. Nor would any class have a monopoly of public offices; instead, all citizens were to be eligible to help govern themselves.[5]

The republican ideal, in other words, implied political equality. As Simeon Baldwin suggested, in a republic there "must . . . be as little subordination as the Nature of government will admit." [6] Thus republicanism renounced the props which governments traditionally had relied on to maintain themselves: privileged classes and rulers chosen by the Lord.

Republicans had a striking substitute for the old means. They were willing to gamble their entire political experiment on the belief that education could equip men to rule themselves. "Education," according to Baldwin, "may . . . be admitted . . . as the only support of this form of Gov't—for the Souls of Individuals thus expanded are from the noblest principles attached to the Interest of the State—feel themselves infinitely above the bribes of the rich—are Emulous for the attainment of Office by their superior merits in knowledge, Virtue & Love of Mankind." [7] Dependent upon its citizens, any one of whom might be summoned to office, a republic was compelled by simple prudence to educate them. Republicanism did not prescribe any specific curriculum, as far as one can judge from the writings of Baldwin and others: what it required was that education help provide enlightened and virtuous citizens—not a small task even by the optimistic standards of the day.[8]

5. Republican thought in New England can be examined in many sources, among them *Boston Magazine,* Feb., March, May, July, Nov., 1784 ("The Free Republican"); *Boston Gazette and Country Journal,* May 23, 1785; *Connecticut Gazette* (New London) Mar. 19, 1795.

6. Simeon Baldwin to James Kent, Oct. 16, 1782, Baldwin Family Papers, Yale.

7. Ibid.

8. Ibid. See also the following in which the indispensability of education to a republic is argued: "An Address to the Candidates for the Degree of Bachelor of Arts delivered July 1786" (in the handwriting of Simeon Baldwin), Baldwin Family Papers; *Boston Magazine,* Mar. 1784 ("On Education"); *Massachusetts Centinel,* Mar.

We cannot entirely account for the enormous confidence republicans showed in learning and human ability. Learning, of course, had always commanded the respect of Puritan New England. But Puritans, convinced that Adam's fall had irretrievably tarnished man's reason, had not accorded human faculties the same respect they had given learning. Puritanism faded, however, and as it did, its grim portrait of man lost its hold. American experience with all its practical demands, with its urgency to solve the problems of an expanding society, made the blackness of the old psychology irrelevant. For Americans solved their problems and thereby demonstrated the resources of human talent; and though ministers in New England bewailed a putative degeneracy which, they insisted, accompanied their people's success, they acquiesced in success—indeed, in the jeremiad they developed a literary form which released the communal tension created as New England strayed from its errand into the wilderness. In this way ministers themselves helped free New Englanders from restraint, thus keeping them on their self-chosen road of economic and secular advance. Though this release from guilt may not have reinforced an optimistic view of human nature, it did nothing to lessen it. Economic success and political growth in the eighteenth century, culminating in the Revolution, further disposed New Englanders to think well of man. And, finally, in Locke's *Essay Concerning Human Understanding*—with its optimistic implications—they found psychological confirmation for their beliefs.[9]

After the Revolution their view of man suggested that from birth and through childhood the mind was plastic. Early experi-

---

22, 1786, Mar. 14, 1787, June 4, 1788, Dec. 5, 1795, Sept. 19, 1798; *Newport Mercury*, July 23, 1792. An anonymous writer in *New Haven Gazette and Connecticut Magazine*, May 11, 1786, challenges one of the postulates of republicanism—"Equality is the soul of a republic"—and argues that equality is possible only if all property is held in common, an idea he deplores but which others in Connecticut held.

9. This paragraph is based largely on my own reading of a variety of sources—newspapers, magazines, letters, diaries, and sermons. The last two books of Perry Miller's *From Colony to Province* (Cambridge, Mass., 1953) gave my thinking its initial direction. See chap. 2 of Miller's book for a discussion of the jeremiad.

ence—whether education or something less formal—shaped it, provided habits of thought, and directed its development toward good or evil. Estimates varied as to the extent of its plasticity and as to how completely it could be molded. Those who brought literal-mindedness to Locke described an unlimited role for education, as in the case of the writer who declared "the mind of man at his birth is a perfect blank, on which, as on white paper, the hand of education may write philosopher, statesman, divine, mechanic, bean, or blockhead." Naive environmentalism of this sort did not persuade many. Most subscribed to a view which, while not discounting greatly the pliability of the mind, did insist that it contained certain latent tendencies, both for good and evil. Their exact character was never clearly described, but the task assigned education was clear: it was to develop those good, though dormant, qualities helpful to the individual and the community, and to repress the others.[10]

The optimism stimulated by this psychology and by ebullient republicanism left no doubt that education could meet the challenge. Advocating a college education for all, a writer hoped for "many a Ritenhouse among our Mechanick genii & an American Cincinnatus upon every farm." [11] Others suggested that the Negro—who had never received much education even in New England—could be improved greatly if sent to school. All would have agreed with the writer who insisted that "from no savage shore, is that man to be produced, whom education would not improve." [12]

Agreed on the power of education to shape the plastic mind, New Englanders divided over the forms they desired to give it. The central dispute concerned the classical curriculum: for the

10. The quotation is from *Oracle of the Day*, Oct. 6, 1798. This paragraph is based on *Gentlemen and Ladies Town and Country Magazine*, Oct. 1789; *Newport Mercury*, July 1, 1794; *Massachusetts Magazine*, 2, 275–77 (May 1790); *Massachusetts Centinel*, Sept. 22, 1784, Dec. 5, 1795; *New Haven Gazette*, Apr. 3, 1788.

11. Simeon Baldwin to James Kent, Oct. 16, 1782, Baldwin Family Papers.

12. The quotation is from *Newport Mercury*, July 1, 1794. The suggestion that Negroes should be educated was made in *Massachusetts Centinel*, Sept. 22, 1784.

first time in the century its relevance for American boys was challenged. As in an English dispute of the seventeenth century its defenders and attackers grouped themselves as "ancients" and "moderns," though different issues were involved. The argument in England had been over the new science; in New England, where in the late eighteenth century no one challenged the validity of the scientific outlook, the question turned on what was desirable in education. The ancients were quite willing to settle for the traditional liberal education of colonial days: mathematics, a little natural philosophy, and all the knowledge of the classical languages that could be crammed into a boy's head. With some exceptions moderns were not hostile to science and mathematics, but they were eager to substitute for Latin and Greek more "useful" learning.[13]

There were no formal groupings of ancients and moderns and, as far as one can tell, no informal clubs or associations organized around the issue. The appelations, "ancients" and "moderns," simply refer to writers in the public press who divided on the subject of learning and its relation to their culture. They did not divide along class or occupational lines except in the case of ministers, who probably tended to be ancients through temperament and training. Yet knowledge of the classics did not distinguish ancients from moderns; John Adams, a learned man and a first-rate classicist, was a modern.[14]

Moderns, of course, did not think of themselves as classicists even when they were. They prided themselves on being practical men, and certainly they exhibited interest only in the concrete and immediate. They distrusted "speculation"—a word that seldom appeared in their writings without "idle" appended to

13. The battle of the books in England can best be approached through William Temple, *Of Ancient and Modern Learning* (1690), William Wotton, *Reflections upon Ancient and Modern Learning* (1694), and Jonathan Swift, *The Battle of the Books* (1704). See also Richard F. Jones, *Ancients and Moderns: A Study of the Background of the Battle of the Books* (St. Louis, 1936).

14. Adams did not, however, take part in the controversy discussed below. For a brief statement of his views on the kind of education the new Republic required see C. F. Adams, ed., *Letters of John Adams to His Wife* (2 vols. Boston, 1891), 2, 68.

it. They judged most actions and ideas by their utility. Something was useful if it produced a valuable result—say wealth, or crops, or goods—an idea, if it increased knowledge or understanding that could be applied to the affairs of the ordinary world. For example, a discovery in astronomy which led to improved navigation had greater value than one which gave insight into the nature of the universe but which had no immediate application. John Adams exposed the source of this preoccupation with utility when he remarked: "It is not indeed the fine arts which our country requires; the useful, the mechanic arts, are those which we have occasion for in a young country." [15] Here was the key—America was young and still to be built; and moderns dedicated to the vision of a new, unique America could not contain their impatience with anything that did not contribute to the building.[16]

Hence, learning for itself did not interest moderns, only its application. And the wider the application the more useful the learning. The trouble with classical learning, they liked to say, was that it was useful only to the clergy. And moderns tended to be contemptuous of the clergy, if not actually anticlerical. Thus one man could comment that the "clergy had no business, [and] their science had no object." [17] But moderns did not object to Latin and Greek simply because ministers admired them. The more compelling reason was that the languages had no utility in the growing Republic. Why, they scoffed, give would-be merchants and artisans Latin and Greek that they would never use and probably forget immediately after they left school. Give a boy knowledge which, unlike Roman oratory, would help him behind a shop counter.[18]

Education for them was supremely useful if it prepared a boy to earn his living. They believed that individual and nation alike

15. Ibid.
16. *Massachusetts Magazine*, 1, 746–49 (Dec. 1789). *New Haven Gazette and Connecticut Magazine*, June 12, 19, 1788. *Connecticut Courant*, May 11, 1795.
17. *New Haven Gazette*, Mar. 16, 1791. See also *Massachusetts Magazine*, 1, 746–49 (Dec. 1789).
18. *Massachusetts Magazine*, 1, 382 (June 1789).

benefited from vocational training. What could be more useful than citizens who worked in occupations for which they had been trained and who thereby contributed to the building of America? In this scheme of things education would function within a restricted compass, simply enabling a boy to fulfill a predetermined role but not liberating his mind or talents in any significant way. All a boy had to do was to choose his occupation; after this initial decision his studies were to be shaped to prepare him to work efficiently in his calling. Such a system, apparently indifferent to the individual, seems admirably suited to the preservation of the status quo. And in a sense it was, but the moderns' claim that boys should be free to choose their own careers was a liberating idea.[19]

Complaints that the classical languages were inappropriate to vocational training did not exhaust the moderns' criticism of them. A few also viewed the languages as a threat to American equality. Not everyone, this minority argued, could hope to learn the languages; consequently knowledge of them became a "badge of distinction."[20] Intellectual superiority apparently could not be tolerated in a republic. In the ominous phrase of one, Americans were "like men" and evidently should always remain so.[21]

A mere excision of the classical languages did not satisfy moderns. They prescribed a curriculum which they expected would produce fervent Americans and republicans. Besides the necessary vocational subjects, every boy should receive instruction in the English language, and American history and geography. Some believed that such a course could not fail to make good patriots; others, not willing to leave anything to chance, insisted that these subjects should be taught so as deliberately to foster American national feeling. All agreed that however

19. *New Haven Gazette*, Mar. 16, 1791. *Massachusetts Magazine*, 7, 204 (July 1795); 8, 529–35 (Oct. 1796); 8, 659 (Dec. 1796).
20. *Massachusetts Magazine*, 8, 535 (Oct. 1796); see also 7, 205 (July 1795).
21. Ibid., 1, 382 n. (June 1789).

pursued, one of the aims of education should be to produce boys devoted to America and its institutions.[22]

While moderns reproached them for their devotion to the impractical and, what was worse, their commitment to the useless, the ancients hardly murmured. Their silence bespoke reluctant agreement; bewildered, one suspects, by all the shouting and perhaps by the demand for practical men in the new nation, they must have wondered if, after all, the classical languages had relevance for America. Of those who spoke out, some were reduced to answering that knowledge of the classical languages helped in learning English, which was true but open to the objection that most people could learn all the English they ever needed by studying it alone. Only an occasional ancient argued that genuine intellectual effort fed on all kinds of nourishment and could not be diverted by the claims of utility. One who did also charged that "the short-sighted and superficial reasoners of the present day, will not allow any merits or importance in pursuits, of which the utility is not immediately placed before their eyes." This same writer also maintained that study of the classics was justified by the pleasure it gave, a view many ancients probably subscribed to but hesitated to express.[23]

The shape to be given to young minds was not the only educational issue troubling New Englanders. Where the shaping should occur was a question they also began to discuss. Should it be in the public-supported grammar schools, or in the academies that had sprouted all over New England after the Revolution? Since virtually all academies gave instruction in the classical languages, they competed with the grammar schools for students. In this competition some exponents of the town grammar schools, including Governor Samuel Adams of Massachu-

22. *New Haven Gazette*, Mar. 16, 1791. *Massachusetts Magazine*, 1, 381–83 (June 1789).

23. The quotation is from *New Haven Gazette*, Mar. 16, 1791. For the argument that the classics increased one's knowledge of English see *Massachusetts Magazine*, 8, 420–23 (Aug. 1796); also ibid., 2, 160–62 (Mar. 1790).

setts, perceived a threat to free public education. Because they were private and therefore at least theoretically exclusive, the academies, they feared, would appeal to the rich; and if the rich sent their children to private schools, they would not wish to support the public schools. Deprived of their support, town schools would surely fail, and with their failure learning would become the monopoly of the few. The poor, unable to send their children to the academies, would sink into ignorance. And the rich as the only educated group would become an aristocracy, with fatal results for the Republic.[24]

Without bothering to refute this prediction specifically, academy-founders, trustees, and legislatures, which often chartered the academies, all proclaimed their allegiance to the Republic. The critics of academies, they evidently believed, had missed the point. For if learning was indispensable to a republic, why not propagate it in every possible way, in private as well as public schools? [25]

Even with Samuel Adams on their side, the enemies of academies were weak and apparently few in number. Their significance lay not in their achievement, or lack of it, but in the illustration they once again provided of the widespread presumption that republicanism rested on an educated people.

As the discussion of the relative merits of public and private schools left New England's people unmoved, so also did the controversy between ancients and moderns. Perhaps one dispute diminished the force of the other. In any case neither seriously affected public policy, though Samuel Adams blocked incorporations of Massachusetts academies during his tenure as governor.

24. "On Education," MSS endorsed "Written by a well wisher, to his fellow countryman [sic], Acton, May 12, 1789 of Middlesex" [Massachusetts], in Penniman MSS Collection, Yale. *Massachusetts Centinel,* Mar. 22, 1786, Mar. 7, 1787, Aug. 8, 1789. *Boston Magazine,* Mar., Apr., June 1784. *Massachusetts Magazine, 8,* 159 (Mar. 1796).

25. For a brief defense of private schools see *Massachusetts Magazine, 7,* 205–06 (July 1795).

Nor did ideas proposed outside New England alter public policy or, for that matter, shape the debate. Almost a generation before the Revolution, ferment in educational ideas occurred elsewhere, especially in Pennsylvania. Benjamin Franklin, as one would expect, proposed the most far-reaching innovations in education. Franklin's ideas were the consequence of his central social perception: the world was in flux in directions which could rarely be predicted. Somehow education must prepare one for change; and it must be prefatory to further learning and change, for Franklin saw life as a process of continual reconstruction. His own had been so—his conceptions of education owed much to his experience.

Not even the academy Franklin proposed for Pennsylvania could give boys *"every Thing* that is useful, and *every Thing* that is ornamental,"* but it could teach "those Things that are likely to be *most useful* and *most ornamental*." [26] Franklin's prescriptions for curricula show that he thought that many subjects could be useful and ornamental to boys. Every boy should be able to read well, of course, and training in speaking and writing were almost as important. Natural history, arithmetic, geography, geometry, accounts, and English grammar should be taught. After that the curriculum might be adapted to some extent to the needs of a particular profession; boys who intend to enter the ministry, for example, should learn Latin and Greek; those heading for the practice of medicine should study French as well.

If Franklin's theory conceived of education as a process by which skills and knowledge were imparted, it also emphasized the need to produce a moral and social attitude in young men, the idea of service to "Mankind, one's Country, Friends and Family." Many subjects provided an opportunity for introducing such ideas, and Franklin urged that no opportunity be lost. The study of natural history, for example, could be improved

26. This quotation and those in the next paragraph are from "Proposals Relating to the Education of Youth in Pennsylvania" in Leonard Labaree, ed., *The Papers of Benjamin Franklin* (New Haven, 1961), 3, 397–421.

by putting boys to practicing "a little Gardening, Planting, Grafting, Inoculating." After all, the "Improvement of Agriculture" was "useful to all." But it was in the study of history that Franklin perceived the greatest opportunities for introducing other ideas: geography, chronology, ancient customs, morality, oratory, "public religion," politics, languages, commerce, mechanics—all might be approached through its broad doors. Morality, for example, would appear necessary to a student if introduced by "Observations on the Causes of the Rise or Fall of any Man's Character, Fortune, Powere, &c mentioned in History. . . . Indeed the general natural Tendency of Reading good history must be, to fix in the Minds of Youth deep Impressions of the Beauty and Usefulness of Virtue of all Kinds, Publick Spirit, Fortitude, &c."

All this implied change in pedagogy. If history was to be used as an opening into almost all other subjects, the old formal distinctions would have to be abandoned. Franklin's other suggestions about teaching were not new, however. They assumed the familiar things about children: their minds could be strengthened by exercise; they could be stimulated to learn if they competed for prizes; and their desires to imitate and please their teachers could be exploited in the classroom.

New England found it easy to ignore all of Franklin's ideas. When he first wrote about education at the middle of the eighteenth century, his proposals may have appeared to be directed to Pennsylvania alone. In any case, New Englanders did not consider altering them to fit their society. After the Revolution, Franklin's suggestions probably seemed even less adaptable, for they did not employ the republican vocabulary, nor did they appear to be addressed to republican problems.

All this should not be taken as evidence that intellectuals had lost their power to influence public action in New England. They remained a potent force long after the Revolution, especially when they agreed among themselves. But except for the conviction that education was essential to a republic, little agreement existed among them. Displayed in the press, their disputes could not have escaped the eye of the public.

Though New England chose not to embark the state on a deliberate course of educational change, change nevertheless occurred after the Revolution in curriculum and in institutions. And the state took part. But its action came as a result of a set of conditions which had nothing to do with the debate over public and private education.

9. Vanishing Grammar Schools

THE public-supported grammar schools found living through the rhetoric of the moderns easier than surviving the Revolution. For battle destroyed schoolhouses as readily as other property, and armies claimed schoolmasters as eagerly as other citizens. Even if their school buildings escaped destruction, some towns, pressed by the need to outfit and pay troops, closed their schools and permitted the problems of education to vanish from the discussions in their meetings. Probably more kept their schools open. Towns remote from the fighting or with endowments had the easiest time. Many without these special sources of income but with resources even more valuable—citizens determined to preserve education whatever the hardships—somehow found money for both war and education.[1]

After the Revolution, New Englanders returned to their customary concerns and their usual mode of operations in government and education. Just as before the Revolution, school committees or selectmen hired masters, put up buildings, and did all the numerous chores connected with running a school. Taxation and private donations continued to furnish almost all the income required to run the schools.

Some communities made changes in administrative techniques. Boston, which had always relied upon its selectmen, decided in 1789 to appoint a school committee to assist in the affairs of education. In the 1790s this group took almost complete direction of the schools into its own hands, but made no drastic change in school policy. The city revised its school system at the same time—the most important change being the elimina-

---

1. This paragraph is based on town records and local histories cited throughout.

tion of one grammar school. Educational policy remained in the care of the meeting itself.[2]

The most significant change made before the end of the century in the administration of secondary education occurred in Massachusetts with the Education Act of 1789.[3] As in all previous ones, the act placed responsibility with the towns for the maintenance of grammar schools. But it authorized them to form school districts to carry out most educational functions. Districts, the act made plain, were the solution to the old problem of a scattered town population which had made education so difficult to provide. Many towns had resorted to a division of responsibility such as the act now authorized, long before the Revolution. The statute simply recognized the validity of the traditional mechanisms. Districts were not authorized to tax; their financial support was to come from the town meeting. Nor were they intended to maintain grammar schools; that responsibility continued to lie with the town. A second provision of the act required only towns of two hundred families to maintain grammar schools, a change that legally freed 117 towns of the expense of a Latin master. The only other part of the statute directly related to the grammar school ordered that no scholar was to be admitted until he had demonstrated ability to read English.

At the time of its passage the act aroused little criticism. By authorizing towns to set up school districts, it attempted to end the problems a centralized system presented for a dispersed population. Townsmen of the outskirts now had hope of getting their children into a school regularly without the strain of long travel. The entrance requirement seemed to be an attempt to restore the grammar school to its traditional function of training Latin scholars and no others. And the two-hundred-family requirement must have pleased taxpayers inordinately.

2. *Reports of the Record Commissioners*, 31, 218.
3. The act is in *Acts and Laws of the Commonwealth of Massachusetts* [1788–89] (Boston, 1894), pp. 416–21.

Critics of the act appeared in the nineteenth century, the most notable being Horace Mann. At the time he became Secretary of the Massachusetts Board of Education, the worst effects of the act were apparent: the two-hundred-family requirement had cut down the number of schools drastically, the administration of school districts was marked by indifference, and existing tax funds were so widely dispersed by the division of responsibility among school districts that only a rare district had money enough to do its job adequately.[4]

Although Mann's complaints concerned early nineteenth-century education, at least one of the defects he noted appeared immediately after the passage of the law of 1789. The number of schools fell disastrously to about half the colonial number. Before the Revolution, in an ordinary year, about sixty-five Massachusetts schools opened their doors to grammar scholars. In the 1790s only thirty taught the languages, despite the fact that there were 110 towns with at least two hundred families.[5] The law provided that towns delinquent in furnishing a grammar school were to be fined thirty pounds, but the courts did not collect the penalty.[6]

In Connecticut during most of the period before the end of the century the three old schools in New Haven, Hartford, and New London and the newcomer, Danbury, continued along familiar administrative ways. The Hartford board of trustees maintained its customary close watch. So tight was the Hartford board's grip on the affairs of the school that the master in 1790 had to secure its permission merely to substitute a late edition of Jedidiah Morse's *Geography* for the one then in use.[7] The trustee also demanded a monthly report from him on the conduct of his scholars. In New London the school committee,

4. Mary Mann, ed., *Life and Works of Horace Mann* (5 vols. Cambridge, 1867–1870), 2, 384–432; 3, 528–29.

5. Bureau of the Census, *Heads of Families at the First Census of the United States Taken in the Year 1790: Massachusetts* (Washington, D.C., 1908).

6. *Acts and Laws*, p. 419.

7. Hartford Grammar School Records, meeting Jan. 6, 1790, CHS.

as it had for years, gave an annual accounting of the grammar school financial holdings. And the town itself demonstrated its traditional interest in education—sometimes tangibly, as in 1788, when it directed that the money obtained from the sale of a town-owned ferry house go to the grammar school.[8]

New Haven's Hopkins emerged shakily from the war, unable to keep its doors open regularly until 1786. In the two or three years preceding, inflation and confusion as to the resources the school could depend upon inhibited its operation. And in the two years afterward, though Hopkins taught boys just as it always had, financial stability eluded the school. But in the 1790s the school operated in a fashion calculated to satisfy the most demanding trustees: it stayed within its annual budget (except for two years); it opened regularly; it never lacked a master; and it improved its building—all this without diminishing its endowment by a penny.[9] Expenses were not great, never going over £125; and the trustees were able to assess tuition when additional income seemed necessary.[10] This they did in 1786 and again in 1798, when faced with an irate master who demanded a larger salary.[11] Most years the school's expenses were so low that not even moderate tuition was necessary.

The return of economic stability permitted a gratifying discovery: the school's endowment had come through the Revolutionary period virtually intact. For years no one was certain how the school's investments would fare in the economic disorder of the war and its aftermath. Just before revolutionary agitation began in 1764, Hopkins held assets valued at £819. Not until 1789 did the trustees learn that the war had diminished this sum by only £25.[12]

Change in Connecticut's system came in the middle 1790s.

8. New London Town Meeting Records, Dec. 15, 1788, City Clerk's Office.

9. Records of the Hopkins Grammar School, 2, passim (pagination uncertain), New Haven.

10. Expenses in 1795 were £122 4s. 10 1/2d.

11. Records of the Hopkins Grammar School, 2, meetings of Sept. 25, 1786, Dec. 18, 1798.

12. See the vote ibid., 1, for 1764; and the one in 2, Mar. 6, 1789.

Producing it were a peculiar combination of land, religion, and the traditional concern for education. Land in the West, claimed under the Charter of 1662, supplied the initial spur. Connecticut ceded most of this claim to the federal government in 1786 but thriftily hung onto a large portion. Some of this reserved land it sold, and in 1792 it compensated sufferers from British raids with a grant of a half-million acres.[13] Since the next year seemed to present a good time for disposal of the rest at a profit to the state, the legislature, by a statute subsequently called the "Appropriation Act," [14] directed that the prospective receipts of the sale of western holdings were to go into a perpetual fund. The income from this fund was to be paid to Connecticut churches of all denominations for the support of ministers and schools. At the time the legislature expected that the income earned by the fund would be large enough to give every Connecticut town around $600 a year.

The act was scarcely engrossed when critics filled with both religious and anticlerical fire fell on it. Their chief complaint was that though in theory the income from the fund was to go to churches of all denominations, in fact the orthodox ecclesiastical societies through weight of numbers would control the money. Since they were not disposed to share it, minority churches would sit at a scanty table.[15]

The opposition of such churches was predictable. A second group, shapeless and unorganized, simply opposed giving the money for religious purposes, arguing that other uses were more appropriate—among them education. The issue entered town meetings, inciting at least nine towns to condemn the act. Several also ordered their deputies to work for its repeal.[16]

Conservatives on the Council delayed repeal until the spring of 1795, when a second act directed that the income was to be

13. See the discussion in C. J. Hoadly and Leonard Labaree, eds., *The Public Records of the State of Connecticut*, 8, xiii–xvii.

14. Ibid., pp. 100–01.

15. Ibid., p. xv. *Connecticut Gazette*, Mar. 12, 19, 1795.

16. Hoadly and Labaree, 8, xiv.

paid to school societies, which were to use it for education.[17] A school society, a local unit that included voting members of all the churches in the district whatever their religious denomination, had the option, if two-thirds of its members desired and the legislature approved, to apply any portion of its share of the land's income to the ministry. Division of the money among the various churches of the district was to be in proportion to their respective memberships. (No society ever made such an appropriation despite this provision of the act.) [18]

Though the funds were granted to the school societies, responsibility for secondary education was not placed with them until 1798. By the terms of an act of that year and a second one in 1799, a society was permitted to institute "a School of a higher Order"—the older grammar school under a new name.[19] These acts marked the end of the old policy of compulsion, since no society had to maintain such a school against its members' wishes. Societies were quick to inaugurate new schools and continue old ones, but few schools offering the languages appeared in the closing days of the eighteenth century.

New Hampshire, too, reshaped its educational policy after the Revolution. The fifty-family requirement, the state evidently believed, was not stiff enough. So, in a statute of 1789 it ordered every town and parish to keep an English grammar school.[20] Such a school had to teach reading, writing, and arithmetic. The same act decreased local responsibility for maintaining Latin schools. Now, only shire and half-shire towns were to support such schools. The act also established the authority of selectmen to tax polls and estates for educational expenses. Some of the bite of older laws was retained in the provision

17. Ibid., pp. 237–39.

18. Ibid., pp. 238–39.

19. For the Act of 1798 see ibid., 9, 178–81. For the one of 1799, ibid., pp. 344–49. For the quotation, ibid., p. 180.

20. The statute is in Henry Harrison Metcalf, ed., *Laws of New Hampshire* (7 vols. Bristol and Concord, 1916), 5, 449–50.

which provided that selectmen could be compelled to pay out
of their own pockets any sum they failed to raise. And in a
step to improve teaching, the act required that every master be
certified by "an able master" and a minister, or an academy
preceptor, or a president of a college.[21]

The act released most towns from their old responsibilities to
secondary education. For in the 1790s there were only five
counties in the state, each, of course, with a shire town. Two
had two half-shire towns each; and so the grand total of towns
required by law to offer classical instruction was nine.[22]

Unlike the school laws of New Hampshire's colonial period,
this one was observed. For at least three of the shire towns—
Dover, Exeter, Keene—all that had to be done was simply to
continue schools of long standing. This they did. Dover not only
supported a grammar school but somehow found money for
a system of district schools.[23] Exeter also financed more than
one school, apparently put up at least one additional school
building, and explored new ways of administering the school
system. During most of the earlier period the town meeting
had made most decisions regarding education, and the selectmen
had carried them out. In the 1790s the town resorted to special
committees; one charged with inspection was organized annually
from 1792 on, and in 1795 it was given authority to regulate
all school affairs. The town, of course, could call it to account,
change its personnel, or dismiss it at any time.[24] The two remaining shire towns—Haverhill and Nashua—may not have
followed the new law as closely as the other three, but both
maintained schools through the 1790s.[25]

21. Ibid., 5, 449.

22. Ibid.

23. Dover Town Records, Petition to Selectmen, Feb. 29, 1796, Town Meeting,
Mar. 29, 1796, Microfilm, New Hampshire State Library.

24. Exeter Town Records. For the new school see meeting of Mar. 9, 1795. For the
committee of 1792, meeting Mar. 27, 1792; committee's strengthened authority,
Mar. 9, 1795. Microfilm, New Hampshire State Library.

25. Haverhill Town Records and Nashua Town Records. Microfilm, New Hampshire State Library.

The half-shire towns did almost as well. Portsmouth of Rockingham County had the oldest grammar school in the state. Like almost every other school in New England, it had always received readers and writers as well as Latin scholars, and had relied upon a single master to teach both groups. But just before passage of the new law the town decided to deny entrance to all scholars except those "forward enough to enter upon the Study of the English Language grammatically." [26] It also required each scholar to have a grammar and a dictionary. Four years later it hired an usher, who was to assist the master in instructing a greater number of students. Up to this time the curriculum had included only English, writing, and arithmetic besides the learned languages. With an usher the town was hopeful that the master might add geography, geometry, philosophy, chronology, history, biography, logic, and rhetoric.[27]

With no public provision for education, Rhode Island was not concerned about reforming school laws. She was indeed not at all interested in establishing a state-wide system of public-supported education. A few proposals for such a move were brought forward after the Revolution but made no headway.[28]

The old town grammar schools in Providence and Newport and a few other places continued to open. As before the Revolution, Providence helped maintain a handsome brick schoolhouse and furnished a school committee staffed by important citizens to inspect its classes. But the town contributed little direction and less money.[29]

Newport furnished the one bright spot in an otherwise dismal picture. Its grammar school remained open throughout the century—even though the city, with its economy gradually declining, had less and less money to spend. Elsewhere little was

26. Portsmouth Town Records, Mar. 25, 1789. Microfilm, New Hampshire State Library.

27. Ibid., Mar. 26, 1793.

28. *Providence Gazette*, Feb. 15, 22, 1794. *Newport Mercury*, July 23, 1792.

29. *Providence Gazette*, June 12, 1790; Apr. 2, Oct. 1, 1791; Mar. 30, Nov. 9, 1793; Jan. 4, 1794; Oct. 15, 1796; Apr. 1, 1797.

done, and education in Rhode Island remained, as one of her citizens complained, "too much neglected." [30]

The complaint, of course, might have been made of all New England, for a desire to lessen the burden of public-supported education existed in every state. All responded to this desire— by lessening the local requirement, as in Massachusetts and New Hampshire, or by tapping western lands in order to relieve taxation, as in Connecticut.

At first sight, New Englanders' reluctance to grant public money for schools seems to mock their protestations of devotion to education. Yet they meant it when they said that a republic rested on an educated people, and they were sincere when they praised education on other counts.

Not only did they praise education, they acted to provide it. They hired more private masters than ever before, and established academies with fat endowments, fine buildings, and complicated administrative apparatus. In short, their zeal for education seems to have been greater than ever, but it was a zeal now channeled into private education.

This would seem to suggest that the multiplication of these private facilities sent the public-supported grammar schools into a decline. But this hypothesis reverses the sequence of events— for in fact the new private schools filled a void left by the vanishing town schools. The sequence was especially clear in Massachusetts and New Hampshire, where academies did not appear in large numbers until after passage of the acts of 1789 reducing the local educational requirement. Academies appeared earlier in Connecticut—immediately after the Revolution—because the slender public support given education there invited private contributions. [31]

Town-supported schools disappeared not because of competition of academies but because local communities wanted to be rid of them. They were a burden, a drain on taxes, in a com-

30. *Providence Gazette*, Feb. 22, 1794.
31. Academies are discussed below, Chap. 10.

munity that felt crushed by taxes. Besides, there was the debt incurred during the Revolution which each year consumed huge interest charges even after the federal government assumed the burden of part of it. In Massachusetts, for example, annual interest charges in 1786 were $278,700; in 1794, $114,900.[32] Under such demands the allocation of public resources became wedded everywhere in New England to the principle of frugality. In Massachusetts, the Handlins tell us, "a tacit agreement" existed that property taxes would have to decrease.[33] The result was that the yearly state tax remained at the same level, $133,000, throughout the period 1795–1820.[34]

As in the states, debt was a normal burden in many towns. They naturally looked for relief wherever they could find it. For education the result was obvious: the old commitment was not repudiated, but it was diminished.

Though by the end of the century the public-supported grammar school was a vanishing institution, internally it resisted change. As in the colonial period a single master taught all the students and disciplined the unruly. But if he was wise, he did not deceive himself with the thought that he was the real governor of the school. For control remained with the town, which through its meeting periodically appointed committees to supervise the school. Dominated by men of position and wealth, the committee's membership was indistinguishable from earlier colonial bodies. In functions, too, it resembled the old colonial group. In these unspectacular ways the tradition of external control continued and the dependence of the school on the community remained, though the community itself no longer relied so completely on the public-supported grammar school.

32. Oscar and Mary Handlin, *Commonwealth, A Study of the Role of Government in the American Economy: Massachusetts, 1774–1861* (New York, 1947), p. 66 n.
33. Ibid., p. 65.
34. Ibid.

10. The Emergent Academy

As public education declined, New Englanders turned increasingly to small private schools. But useful as they were in providing vocational training, these institutions proved unable to fill the gap left by the vanishing town schools. As before the Revolution, their masters tended to flock to the larger towns, where opportunities were greater. In the competition of the open market, a school had to offer more than Latin and Greek in order to attract students. Instruction in the languages accordingly suffered.

What was worse, small schools continued to be transitory affairs—here today while their masters looked for something better and gone tomorrow when they found it. This was true despite a growing tendency among masters to seek the patronage of local worthies. Even a group as distinguished as the one that sponsored Jedidiah Morse in New Haven in 1785 could not guarantee institutional permanence. Morse's patrons included a judge, Charles Chauncy; a prominent merchant and local official, Henry Daggett; a physician, Ebenezer Beardsley; and New Haven's postmaster-merchant, Elias Beers.[1] Probably because of this group's sponsorship, the school enjoyed great success, drawing so many students that Morse had to hire an assistant.[2] These men lent their names, but they failed to organize a governing body that might have hired another master when Morse left the classroom for the pulpit in 1786.

If the gap left by failing town schools was to be filled, obvi-

1. *New Haven Gazette,* Apr. 21, 1785. To identify several of Morse's patrons I have used Rollin G. Osterweis, *Three Centuries of New Haven, 1638–1938* (New Haven, 1953), and Dexter, *Biographical Sketches of the Graduates of Yale.*

2. Jedidiah Morse to his father, Apr. 12, 1785, Morse Family Papers, Yale.

ously what was needed was not more schools like Morse's but an institution able to command private support and to survive the deaths and departures of masters. The academy arose in answer to this need.

Before the Revolution an occasional private school styled itself "academy." To people who knew the classics or knew of them, as most New Englanders did, the name carried prestige— though the schools adopting it differed in no important way from dozens of others less pretentiously designated. After the Revolution, however, academies that boasted genuine differences from ordinary private schools appeared in New England. And by the end of the century schools were calling themselves academies in an attempt to clothe themselves in the prestige earned by their predecessors of the eighties and nineties.[3]

For the academy in these years became the most important kind of institution providing secondary education. How did it differ from any other private school? After reading the newspaper advertisements of some, it is possible to conclude that an academy was simply a small school giving itself airs. But this is not fair; most of the schools calling themselves academies did differ in significant ways from the small private schools. For one thing, an academy developed an institutional life that survived the turnover of its teachers. Even Lebanon Academy, which came to be closely identified with Nathan Tisdale, its master for twenty years, had begun forty years before he took it over and continued several years after his death. And when Timothy Dwight left Greenfield, his famous academy continued under Jeremiah Day, who also succeeded him at Yale.[4]

Neither Greenfield nor Lebanon was incorporated. Though both lasted longer than most private schools, the life of each might have been prolonged by incorporation, for a charter from a state government always established a self-perpetuating board of trustees much less likely to collapse or die than a single master. Academy founders in Massachusetts and New Hamp-

3. See the newspapers for the last years of the century.
4. *Connecticut Gazette*, May 4, 1787. *Connecticut Journal*, Oct. 29, 1795.

shire were especially aware of this, and most of the academies in those two states were incorporated.

An academy often had a more formal internal organization than smaller schools, which, as we have seen, usually relied on one master to teach all subjects. Plainfield Academy in Connecticut had three departments—English, mathematics, and classics—with a master for each; and Phillips Andover, in an arrangement common to many, boasted a writing master as well as an instructor who taught the classics. Windham Academy in 1785 sported "a qualified Female Instructor of Ladies" besides a preceptor and two ushers.[5] Women instructors were found only in those schools which trained girls as well as boys.[6]

Although organization varied, almost all academies included at least two schools within their doors, an English school teaching children the subjects offered by common schools, and a secondary school supplying about the same training that the free grammar schools gave. Not one seems to have had a vocational department, though several offered practical training of some kind.

In its government, too, the academy differed from the single master school. A private master ordinarily ran his own school to suit himself; in an academy what today is grandly called administration was lifted from the master's shoulders by some sort of board or committee. Charters of incorporation always provided for such a body. Usually the charter named the board of trustees, ordinarily a group ranging in size from about nine to fifteen. The trustees were given power to select their own replacements, to manage the school's income and estate, to elect officials including teachers and assistants, to determine their tenure and duties, and to make rules governing the conduct of officers and students. Restrictions on their authority were few but important: usually they could not move the school, or if

5. *New Haven Gazette,* June 23, 1785.
6. For Plainfield see Ellen D. Larned, *History of Windham County* (2 vols. Worcester, 1880), 2, 322. For Phillips Andover see Jedidiah Morse, *An Address to the Students at Phillips Academy, in Andover* (Charlestown, 1799), v.

they could, only in cases in which more than a majority approved. Sometimes they found that the estate belonging to the school was hedged with restrictions. In Dummer Academy, the trustees knew that should they fail to use the proceeds from the Dummer bequest over a two-year period, it was to revert to Dummer's heirs. Similarly, income from other sources had to be used for the school; Harvard College stood to reap the benefits of a failure extending over two years.[7]

The greatest restriction of all was on the total income permitted an academy. In Massachusetts no academy was ever allowed to hold real estate which returned more than £500 a year or personal estate which yielded more than £2,000. New Hampshire and Connecticut charters imposed similar limits. Such provisions implied no distrust of education; they reflected the common concern that no corporation grow so large as to challenge the state.[8]

In many unincorporated academies, groups similar to official trustees presided. Though they could not claim to be corporations, they could do almost everything a chartered group did. They appointed and removed themselves; they held the purse strings, invested money, hired teachers, put up buildings, and made rules designed to make boys docile and obedient. They called themselves by various names: the groups running Lebanon and Windham were committees, Pomfret's were proprietors (probably because each put up money to be invested in the school), and Granby's were trustees, like any incorporated group.[9]

7. Massachusetts charters are in *Private and Special Statutes of the Commonwealth of Massachusetts, 1780–1805* (3 vols. Boston, 1805). Connecticut charters can be found in the volumes on education in the Connecticut State Archives, CSL. For New Hampshire charters see Metcalf, *Laws of New Hampshire.* For Dummer Academy see *Private and Special Statutes of Mass.,* 1, 33–36, and Harriet W. Marr, *The Old New England Academies* (New York, 1959).

8. See, for example, *Private and Special Statutes of Mass.,* 1, 34, 74, 472; and Metcalf, *Laws of New Hampshire,* 6, 274.

9. For Lebanon see *Connecticut Gazette,* May 4, 1787. For Windham see Trumbull MSS Collection, 2, 77–78, Yale, and *Connecticut Gazette,* June 1, 1787. For Pomfret

The histories of boards of trustees demonstrates the melancholy fact that organization frequently breeds more organization. Trustees could never resist dividing themselves into groups, especially those of Phillips Andover who found an extraordinary number of uses for committees. Theirs were of two types, standing and temporary. The committee of exigencies was a standing body, composed of resident trustees who acted for the trustees when that group was in recess. Discipline apparently proved a serious enough matter to call for a second standing group on expulsions. Its membership fluctuated, though the preceptor always served on it. While the standing committees were formed to meet persistent problems, temporary committees grew as rapidly as problems appeared, and vanished when they fulfilled their purposes. Thus at various times there was a committee to consider a method of appointing trustees, a committee to make up term bills and judge exemptions from payment, a committee to shingle the preceptor's house, a committee to lease the school lands, and a committee to hear petitions for abatement of term charges. The trustees even solemnly appointed a committee to consider a proposal to build outhouses. (One hopes that this committee did not delay action—as committees were prone to do.)[10]

The "better sort of men" tended to sit on such boards—lawyers, physicians, landholders, the distinguished in every field. Often they had contributed to the academy; serving as trustees assured them that they could watch their money being spent. Clergymen sat, too, but they were never a majority on any board—or even a near one. To forestall such a possibility, New Hampshire charters usually contained the provision that of the trustees "a major part shall be Laymen and respectable Freeholders."[11]

see *Connecticut Gazette*, Apr. 30, 1784. For Granby see *Connecticut Courant*, Nov. 17, 1794.

10. Extracts from the Records of Phillips Academy, meetings of Apr. 29, 1778; Apr. 20, 1779; Apr. 18, 1780; Aug. 18, 1781; July 7, 1783; July 12, 1785; Jan. 23, 1786; Feb. 13, 1786; July 9, 1787; July 7, 1789: Park Family Papers, Yale.

11. See, for example, Phillips Exeter's charter, in Metcalf, *Laws of New Hampshire, 4, 372.*

As in most things, getting an academy under way was easy if enough money was available. Phillips Andover and Phillips Exeter had no trouble at all, for Samuel Phillips of Andover and his brother John of Exeter endowed them lavishly. Andover received gifts of $71,000 within a few years of its beginning, and Exeter, $58,000. Although usually of a more modest size, gifts were not uncommon. Lieutenant Governor William Dummer's donation of a house and farm, which started the school still bearing his name in South Byfield, Massachusetts, was about the average size, as was the 400 acres that Staples Academy received in 1781 from Samuel Staples.[12]

Not large gifts from individuals but private groups, willing to give money themselves and willing to seek it from others, started most academies. Such a body served Plainfield Academy well. Numbering nineteen, it was not a large group, nor did it intend originally to create an academy. All it wanted was a school for its members' children. In 1770 the proprietors (as its members called themselves) agreed to build a schoolhouse, a large one for the time, measuring forty-one feet by twenty-four, and a story in height. The middle school district of Plainfield in which the school was to be located, the proprietors decided, should be allowed to send its children as long as it contributed toward the support of the school. But contributions should not qualify the citizens of the district for a voice in the school's proceedings; the proprietors would run the school.[13]

The proprietors put up the bulk of the school's money in amounts as small as fifteen shillings and as large as eight pounds; the total collected amounted to £71 15s. A handsome building of bricks went up, a master took up the ferrule and a Latin grammar, students appeared, and the school prospered even throughout the Revolution. The proprietors may not have always approved of the way things ran, for they soon discovered

12. For the endowments of Phillips Andover and Phillips Exeter see Marr, *Old New England Academies*, p. 3. For the gift to Dummer Academy see *Private and Special Statutes of Mass.*, 1, 33–34, and Marr, ibid., p. 3. For Staples see Conn. Archives, Second Series, 2, 120–25, CSL.

13. Proprietors' Records, Plainfield Academy; see especially the agreement of Oct. 12, 1770, CHS.

that the contributions from the district were accompanied by a claim for a voice in the government of the school. They yielded, and no public squabble ensued.[14]

Success was so great that to receive the increasingly numerous students a second building became necessary by the early 1780s. In 1782 the proprietors authorized its construction, fifty by thirty feet, twelve feet high "between the joints, arched over-head & plastered all over the inside, with suitable seats & Tables, & a Stage, with one porch & two chimneys." [15] To raise the money for the building, the group decided on a public sub-scription, with new proprietors being assessed fifty shillings. Though evidence is lacking as to whether the old proprietors added to these amounts, the records of the group make it clear that they were willing to pay additional sums themselves.[16]

The completed building brought new dignity to the school, or so the proprietors thought, and in the fall of 1782 they de-cided that the school would henceforth be called the "Academy of Plainfield." They named the brick schoolhouse "Coit Hall" after one of the school's chief benefactors. For the new build-ing was reserved the ultimate dignity—it was called Proprietors' Hall.[17]

The proprietors were not satisfied by merely putting up buildings. They knew that institutional permanence required a charter, and this they proceeded to petition for. The Con-necticut Assembly was sympathetic and in 1784 granted them incorporation. The academy now had a promising future.[18]

Other beginnings were less complicated. Leicester Academy was the product of the determination of two men, Ebenezer Crofts of Sturbridge and Jacob Davis of Charlestown, who agreed that central Massachusetts needed an academy. Neither of their home towns appeared to be the right place, but in

14. Ibid., agreement of Oct. 12, 1770, meeting of Feb. 11, 1782. *Providence Gazette,* Oct. 18, 1780; Feb. 3, 1781.

15. Proprietors' Records, Plainfield Academy, meeting of Feb. 25, 1782.

16. Ibid., meetings of Feb. 12, 19, 27, 1782.

17. Ibid., meeting of Sept. 3, 1782.

18. Conn. Archives, Colleges and Schools, First Series, 2, 156, 156a, CSL.

Leicester they discovered a "large and commodious" house.[19] A spacious room on the first floor which had served as a store appeared suitable for a school room and the other rooms could be used by boarding students. Crofts and Davis bought the house, the Leicester town meeting raised £500, and an additional £1,000 was subscribed privately. The General Court acted favorably on a petition for incorporation in 1784, and the academy was underway.[20]

The Leicester town meeting's support of the school was not unusual. In Westfield, Massachusetts, a private group seeking financing for its proposed academy found the town a ready buyer of the shares it issued; and altogether the town raised £300 as a fund for the academy.[21] Towns themselves sometimes took the lead. Gilmantown, New Hampshire, for example, ordered a petition presented to the General Court which set up a private group of trustees like any other similar group. But the town appointed this initial group and determined where the academy was to be built.[22]

Once begun, the problem was how to keep going, a problem that troubled almost every academy at one time or another. Teachers' salaries made up most of a school's annual expenses, but in addition, buildings often required repairs, firewood and candles had to be supplied, and occasionally books needed to be purchased. Exemption from taxation helped academies in Massachusetts, Connecticut, and New Hampshire, but current expenses remained heavy. Permanent or fixed expenses, in particular those connected with buildings, do not seem to have been as difficult to meet. Subscriptions and endowments could usually be raised—probably because buildings were tangible—and could be dedicated to generous donors.

There were a number of sources of income. Every academy charged tuition; some small and unincorporated academies in-

---

19. *Private and Special Acts of Mass.*, *1*, 72.
20. Ibid. Marr, pp. 3–4.
21. *Private and Special Acts of Mass.*, *1*, 454.
22. Metcalf, *Laws of New Hampshire*, 6, 199–201.

deed had no other resources. The going rate for Latin scholars in academies amounted to about one shilling a week in the last two decades of the century. Sometimes it was more, as at Cheshire Academy in 1797, and sometimes less, as at Lebanon in 1787. For the master, teaching and managing his own academy without help, tuition probably was enough. Timothy Dwight's Greenfield Hill, a one-man enterprise for years, brought him £91 in 1781, and Dwight taught only seven students.[23]

Larger schools with several teachers and buildings had to have more money. In Massachusetts they could look to the state for aid. With its large holdings of land in Maine, Massachusetts could afford to be especially generous. Nineteen of the twenty-one Massachusetts academies received state grants of land before the end of the century.[24] Before Dane's Law was passed in 1797 —it provided for a regular procedure to endow academies— the state made grants either at the time of incorporation or by special resolve in answer to petitions. Dane's Law permitted only half-townships to be given; in an obvious attempt to help poor schools the law provided that no academy was to receive land if it already had $3,000. In recognition of the penchant of academy founders to locate their schools in places incapable of supporting them, the law provided that no gift was to be made unless the academy was to be built in a neighborhood of 30,000 to 40,000 inhabitants.[25]

Before this procedure was established, nine academies had persuaded the state to part with some of its land. Seven received whole townships (six miles square), the other two being able to get only half-townships. Several of them sold these lands for prices that the trustees must have found very comforting.

23. Tuition at Cheshire is given in *Connecticut Courant*, Oct. 16, 1797; Lebanon, *Connecticut Gazette*, May, 1787; Greenfield, Stiles Itineraries, 3, 457, Ezra Stiles Papers, Yale.

24. This figure is based on material in *Private and Special Statutes of Mass.*, passim.

25. *Acts and Laws of the Commonwealth of Massachusetts* [1796–97] (Boston, 1896), pp. 307–09.

Leicester's brought $9,000; Marblehead's, $5,600; Hallowell's, $2,099; and most seem to have lent this money out at interest and used the return for all types of expenses.[26]

Connecticut disposed of its western lands in favor of public schools; New Hampshire had none to give; and Rhode Island, preserving its steady indifference to education, gave nothing. Consequently, academies in those states were less handsomely endowed, though private donations took up the slack for some. The 400 acres that Staples Academy received in 1781 rented for about $600 a year in 1805. Windham had no land, but it survived the century through contributions of its owners.[27]

Subscriptions supported by owners, proprietors, and the interested public indeed were an important source. When all these methods failed to raise money, academies sometimes resorted to others. They sold stock, often without very convincing promises of return; and like other entrepreneurs of the early Republic they sometimes resorted to lotteries. Leicester, for example, in 1789 required money for new buildings and for repair of old ones. Deciding on a lottery, the trustees printed 4,000 tickets, which they advertised for sale at two dollars each. Of the total $8,000 which might be realized from the tickets, $6,997 was marked for prizes. Only $1,003 was to go into the academy.[28]

As absorbing a task as it was, the problem of getting money did not occupy all of the trustees' time. Once a master and his assistant had been hired, the trustees had to think about recruiting students. Local reputation, spread by word of mouth, probably served to inform many; but no energetic board depended on it. The newspapers offered more reliable means, and as academies became more numerous and as competition for students increased, trustees advertised frequently and in extravagant detail. Indeed, they made claims for their schools that would have

26. Marr, pp. 20–21.
27. For Staples and Windham see Trumbull MSS Collection, 2, 64, 77.
28. *Massachusetts Centinel*, Sept. 30, 1789, July 28, 1790.

been difficult for a college to live up to. Obviously convinced that extolling the intellectual quality of its academy was not enough, the ordinary board praised anything which might entice students. Plainfield's trustees, for example, reported the location of their academy as most desirable: it was close to the route of public stages and mail arrived six times a week in Plainfield. Then, as now, buildings were important—and the trustees happily testified to the excellence of the academy's. Finally, with an eye on parents, they reported cheap board to be available nearby with respectable families.[29]

After they had persuaded students to attend, the trustees had to look out for them. The master could be counted on to keep them busy during the day, and the trustees rarely interfered with his functions. Books and teaching methods remained entirely under his care, though an occasional board ordered a particular moral tract used. Discipline was another matter: most boards expected their teachers to punish all minor offenses and to see that the scholars observed all the school's regulations. The trustees themselves were usually reluctant to take a hand unless important regulations were violated or in cases in which boys repeatedly offended. The regulations, of course, were a product of the trustees' deliberations; few codes were ever fashioned with more care.[30]

Since every academy claimed to protect the morals of their charges, trustees supervised, inspected, and sometimes licensed houses which lodged and fed students. Most boards insisted that students live only in approved places, whose keepers were expected to abide by the wishes of the academy's governors. In Andover the academy's trustees insisted that no one board more than six boys if other accommodations were available, and that no single lady board more than two.[31] Legally, of course, the

29. *Providence Gazette*, June 16, 1798.

30. See, for example, the Extracts from Records of Phillips Academy, meetings of Apr. 29, 1778; July 7, 1783; July 7, 1789: Park Family Papers.

31. Ibid., meetings of Apr. 18, 1780; July 11, 1791.

trustees could not enforce such regulations, but in practice they found methods of getting their way. They were, after all, important men in their communities, whom boardinghouse keepers hesitated to defy. Usually no trouble arose between the two groups; trustees forestalled it by requiring scholars to obtain permission before they changed their boardinghouses.

In an academy a boy could study all the subjects found in public-supported grammar schools and many others besides. Almost every academy taught the languages, and most also gave instruction in rhetoric, mathematics, geography, English grammar, and the common school subjects—reading, writing, and arithmetic; a few offered logic, natural philosophy, astronomy, and music. About a dozen combined many of these with one or more of the vocational subjects—navigation, surveying, and bookkeeping. And several managed to include the "female branches." [32]

Although by giving this varied curriculum academies served several groups, they were above all classical schools. In their classrooms they received boys striving to become proficient enough to pass college entrance examinations and worked them intensively in the languages. About one hundred and thirty prepared in Lebanon Academy under Nathan Tisdale, for example. [33] Not all of Tisdale's boys entered the freshman classes at Harvard and Yale; a number—especially well taught—were accepted as sophomores and juniors. Other academies prided themselves on giving boys similar training; Timothy Dwight's Greenfield Academy rivaled Yale—even luring boys out of the freshman class, to the discomfort of President Ezra Stiles. [34] Dwight's ambitions irritated the college, but he at least did

32. *Connecticut Gazette*, Apr. 30, 1784. *Connecticut Courant*, June 8, 1784. *Connecticut Journal*, Jan. 7, 1784. *New Haven Gazette*, June 23, Nov. 23, 1785. *Columbian Centinel*, May 25, 1793; June 25, 1796; Aug. 22, 1798. *Providence Gazette*, Aug. 4, 1791; Oct. 11, 1794; June 16, 1798.
33. *Connecticut Gazette*, May 4, 1787.
34. Ezra Stiles, Diary, *10*, 4, 5, 36, Ezra Stiles Papers.

not advertise his intentions in the newspapers, as did John
Bowden of the Episcopal Academy in Cheshire. Bowden in 1787
annoyed the college with his claims that at the academy "the
plan of education is as extensive as that of any College on the
continent." [35]

Despite their grand pronouncements, the academies did not
seriously cut into college enrollments. Some faded quickly.
For example, Abraham Bishop in 1789 interested many citizens
in his proposals for the American Academy in New Haven,
which offered training for children of all ages. He publicized
his plans in a series of pretentious essays published in *The Connecticut Journal* in 1790. His school was to be a model of ef-
ficiency: no longer would students suffer through all subjects
under one master, but would study, say, Latin under one for
an hour or two and on the ringing of a bell would go to another
for geometry. Each Saturday parents would be admitted to see
the students display their learning. Bishop obviously thought
it a grand plan, and it was, but somehow New Haven's citizens
did not appreciate it enough to put up the necessary money,
perhaps because they already had Hopkins, together with an
assortment of private and elementary schools. The result was
that the American Academy, or the Orleans Academy as it
was called in 1790, collapsed after only a few months.[36]

Just as most plans were less ostentatious, so also were most
failures less abrupt. Windham, founded in 1785, stayed open
for about ten years through contributions from its owners. But
in the late 1790s, their purses or their faith depleted, these
men let the school close.[37] Though insolvency accounted for
most closures, there were other reasons. Like every school, an
academy required educated masters, and when it did not obtain
them its reputation diminished. Sharon Academy, which sub-
mitted to a succession of ill-equipped teachers, was branded "no

35. *Connecticut Courant*, Oct. 16, 1797.
36. Bishop's troubles can be followed in *Connecticut Journal*, Jan. 28, 1789; Mar.
10, 17, 24, 31; Apr. 7, 1790; May 5, 1790.
37. Trumbull MSS Collection, 2, 77–78.

more than a common School" by the local minister in 1800—a comment which no doubt hastened its demise.[38]

Even with failures of new attempts like Bishop's and the deaths of older ventures, at least fifty-two academies succeeded after the Revolution. In 1786 Ezra Stiles, commenting that "The Spirit for Academy making is vigorous," listed twelve in Connecticut that had been started in the preceding six years.[39] Two, one at Norwich and one at Stratfield, closed within three years after opening. Most of the others lasted past the end of the century, joined by eight more begun in the nineties.[40]

Massachusetts could count five academies that got their start in the 1780s and at least another sixteen in the 1790s.[41] The lavish state grants of land probably explain this increase just before the end of the century. Neither New Hampshire nor Rhode Island could match that growth, but both had academies. Nine were founded by 1800 in New Hampshire, the most famous being Phillips Exeter.[42] Rhode Island trailed with a handful, two in Newport and one in Providence. The largest and apparently the best was in Newport, headed by Robert Rogers, a graduate and fellow of Rhode Island College. Rogers' Academy demonstrated how pervasive the academy idea was, penetrating even a cultural backwash like Rhode Island. Rogers' school, like almost every academy, offered the familiar cur-

38. Ibid., 2, 23.

39. Stiles, *Literary Diary*, 3, 248.

40. Connecticut academies with dates of their beginnings: Plainfield (1780), Lebanon (1755?), Staples (1781), Pomfret (1782), Lebanon Crank (1782), Greenfield (1783), Stratfield (1783, closed same year), Norwich (1783, closed 1786), Windham (1784), Waterbury (1785), Northbury (1786), Derby (1786), Sharon (1786), American in New Haven (1789, closed 1790), New Milford (1794), Granby (1794), Stanwich (1795?), Federal Academy, Canaan North Society (1795), Stratford (1796), Cheshire (1796), Cornwall (1797).

41. A fairly complete list of Massachusetts academies appears in Marr, pp. 20–21. To this list should be added academies in Dedham and Charlestown—both unincorporated.

42. Besides Phillips Exeter there were academies in New Ipswich (1789), Chesterfield (1790), Charlestown (1791), Atkinson (1791), Amherst (1791?), Haverhill (1793), Gilmantown (1794), and Salisbury (1795).

riculum, boasted its own building, was supervised in part and inspected by a committee of prominent local citizens, and turned out boys prepared for college.[43]

Academies in fact appeared in almost every part of post-Revolutionary America. Moreover, most followed a common pattern—a government vested in laymen established by a charter issued by the state, a financial status dependent upon both public and private contributions, and a curriculum more or less classical.

Their common traits and their spread suggests that academies were institutions created out of conditions existing everywhere in the young Republic. And indeed they were; education everywhere was lacking, and everywhere republican enthusiasm demanded that it be supplied. In New England, where the desire for a decrease in public spending subdued the enthusiasm for knowledge, the academies not only filled a great need but became the means by which the liberal tradition in education was perpetuated.

In its form the academy in New England both broke with the past and continued it, but the break was not striking. To be sure, the academy was a new institution—especially in its size and elaborate structure—but it was improvised from a variety of colonial experiences rather than from fresh ideas about education. Charters, lay groups interested in education, and a curriculum featuring both useful and academic subjects were scarcely new to New Englanders.

Indeed, absence of novelty may have assured success. For along with the old forms and the classical curriculum, the academy inherited a tradition of responsibility to the public. Hence it attempted to purvey not only the learned languages but vocational, elementary, and higher education as well. This was not a light task, and the academy succeeded only imperfectly. It never supplanted parish and town schools, which remained the most important centers of elementary education,

43. *Newport Mercury*, Feb. 13, May 8, June 5, 1786; Aug. 16, 1790; Oct. 1, 1792. *Providence Gazette*, Sept. 13, 1788.

nor did it seriously challenge the colleges which continued to be the centers of higher learning. But on the secondary level the academy proved to be a worthy successor to the grammar school.

Yet its achievement was not an unmixed blessing, for by serving well, the academy also served to diminish the rich potentialities of public-supported education.

11. The Curriculum in the Early Republic

THE American Revolution did not free boys from the tasks colonial masters had long inflicted upon them. A boy beginning the languages learned the rules of grammar, construed and parsed, and recited from memory passages of classical prose and poetry. He made Latin from manuals, sometimes scanned verse, and occasionally tried his hand at composing his own. His knowledge of Greek was scant compared to his command of Latin, but he did work through a grammar and usually the New Testament and one or two other volumes as well. All this was standard colonial practice.

Indeed, few changes—not excepting books—appeared in the classical curriculum. Had a Boston lad of 1712 reappeared in Boston Latin School in the 1790s, about all that he would have noticed amiss was that the scholars now spent four years instead of seven in the school, a change made in 1789. This four-year stint could not match the colonial seven in the number of authors read, but it managed to provide rigorous training in several of the classics. Boys began Latin in a familiar way—with Cheever's *Accidence*. Then it was on to Corderius' *Colloquies*, the *Nomenclature*, Aesop's *Fables*, and Ward's *Latin Grammar*,[1] or Eutropius. In their second year they began Clarke's *Introduction*, continued in Ward and Eutropius, and met such old standbys as Chateillon's *Dialogues* and Garretson's *Exercises*, which they used in making Latin. They enjoyed the delights of Greek grammar for the first time in their third year, read Caesar's *Commentaries*, Ovid, Cicero, and Virgil, and made

1. John Ward, *A Short Introduction of Grammar* (London, 1732).

Latin from King's *Heathen Gods*. In their fourth year they went from Greek grammar to the Greek Testament, continued to make Latin and to read Virgil and Cicero, and began *Gradus ad Parnassum*.[2]

Outside Boston, towns clung to the old curriculum, though in the Hartford Grammar School boys could study navigation, surveying, "or any other branch of the Arts and Sciences" three days a week.[3] But the school's regulations of 1790 prescribed that "The Master shall principally attend to the instruction of his Scholars in the Study of the learned Languages, & of those branches of the arts and Sciences, usually taught in Collegiate Schools."[4] Boys could not even enter the school unless they owned a Latin dictionary, an accidence, a Latin grammar, Corderius, Erasmus, and an English dictionary.[5]

Woburn imposed no such entrance requirement when it reformed its schools in 1792, but its Latin scholars studied from old texts, among others Cheever, Corderius, Chateillon, Ward's *Latin Grammar*, and Clarke's *Introductions to the Making of Latin*. One innovation in the Woburn curriculum appears in the schools' regulations of 1792: the "upper Class" was to pay "attention to English Composition once each week or Fortnight," as the master saw fit.[6] This was an important addition.

If the town-supported grammar schools were addicted to old books and methods, private masters were hardly less so. Even academies followed the old ways. Boys at Sharon Academy in Connecticut, for example, read the familiar classical authors and recited in the traditional manner sometimes twice a day.[7]

Latin scholars in Phillips Academy, Andover, shared the same

2. For the change and the textbooks see *Massachusetts Centinel*, Jan. 9, 1790. See also, *A Volume of Records Relating to the Early History of Boston, Containing Boston Town Records, 1784 to 1796 in Registry Department of the City of Boston: Records Relating to the Early History of Boston*, 21 (Boston, 1903), 208–10.

3. Hartford Grammar School Records, regulations adopted in January, 1790, CHS.

4. Ibid.

5. Ibid.

6. Woburn Town Records, 12, 75–76, Town Clerk's Office.

7. Vinson Gould to Thomas Mills Day, Apr. 13, July 21, Sept. 10, 1794; Jan. 24, 1795. Thomas Mills Day Papers, Yale.

intellectual fare. Indeed, a typical day there was strikingly reminiscent of one in a colonial grammar school. The boys were greeted by Master Eliphalet Pearson at eight o'clock. Religious exercises opened the day, each boy reading a verse aloud from a chapter in the Old Testament. After reading and singing a Psalm, the boys concluded this devotional period with a prayer.

The rest of the morning was spent reciting and studying. Divided into twelve classes, the Academy's fifty-eight scholars, all crowded into a small one-room building, kept Master Pearson's hands full. First he listened to the seven who composed the lowest class. Their lesson consisted of one colloquy in Corderius, from which each boy construed and parsed and spelled a few words—usually no more than four. If there was time in the morning this group recited from a second colloquy. A slightly more advanced class of ten next took up its lesson, a story or two in Aesop's *Fables*. Though they may have paused to savor the charm of the fables, the boys' main business, like that of the beginners, was to learn grammar; hence, their master put them through exercises much like those performed by the first group. He then listened to the third, fourth, and fifth classes work separately through a page or two in Erasmus, construing, parsing, and spelling as they went. Boys in the third and fourth classes recited once each, but the scholars in the fifth were called upon twice. A page and a half diverted the four boys in the sixth class. Like the three in the seventh who recited four pages in Cornelius Nepos, they performed the conventional grammatical exercises. Latin verse occupied the next four classes; the eighth (two boys) worked through seven lines in Ovid; the ninth, twenty lines; the tenth read fifteen or twenty lines in Virgil; and the eleventh, thirty-five or forty. Boys in these classes construed and parsed and spelled as the younger boys did; but since this was verse, they also scanned. By the time he had listened to the eleventh class, the master probably yearned for a change, and he got it when he turned to the seven boys of the twelfth. These lads construed and parsed about sixty verses in the Greek Testament. Their recitation ended a morning which had lasted four long hours, broken only by one ten-minute recess.

After an hour and a half for lunch the entire school, with the exception of the twelfth class, wrote Latin. The seniors, as the twelfth class was called, were directed to construe and parse one hundred lines in Virgil and were also examined in prosody. Writing and recitation lasted ninety minutes; then Pearson "examined" his scholars' Latin prose. Finishing this, he indulgently granted the boys ten minutes of relaxation before starting them on another round of recitation and study. This final period followed the morning schedule except in the case of the seniors, who recited about two pages of Cicero instead of the Greek Testament.

Near the end of the day everybody joined in reading a section in Philip Doddridge's *The Family Expositor,* "accompanied with rehearsals, questions, remarks, & reflections." Then came the singing of a hymn and a prayer and the master dismissed the school—confident, surely, that he and his charges had put in a full day's labor!

Not every day passed in this way. Some days the languages received less attention. On Mondays the master questioned the boys "respecting the public exercises of the sabbath," and on Saturdays he administered punishments. A boy probably welcomed days on which spelling and parsing matches were held and doubtless looked forward to the release afforded when someone caught misbehaving was disciplined before the school.[8]

With fewer scholars than Pearson had at Phillips Academy, private masters operated more simply. Master Thomas Peckham of Newport, for example, boasted in 1789 that he had a new system of teaching Latin. Peckham first put his scholars to writing single Latin words in columns, with their English equivalents beside them. This, according to Peckham, impressed a Latin vocabulary into a lad's mind. After this initial study, his boys went on to Corderius, Eutropius, and Justin. The method,

8. This account and the quotations in the above five paragraphs are from "Memorial to the Trustees," Apr. 17, 1780, Edwards Albert Park Collection, Yale.

Peckham claimed, differed from the "common way," which was
to write "the most trifling Repetition, such as 'Quarrels break
Friendship.' " [9] Despite his brag, his method was not new; colonial masters had directed boys in such tasks, though without
boasting about it.

Peckham's scholars did not read many authors. Few boys did
who studied with private masters. Seeking to qualify their
scholars as quickly as possible for college, such masters worked
their charges intensively in only a few books rather than put
them through a fixed preparatory course. The authors they
chose, of course, were those the colleges customarily examined
in. Though evidence is not plentiful, it seems to indicate that
private masters favored the common texts and editions:
Cheever's *Accidence*, Ward's *Latin Grammar*, Clarke's *Corderius*
and *Introduction to the Making of Latin*, Duncan's *Cicero*,[10]
and Davidson's *Virgil*.[11] Almost any Greek grammar and lexicon seems to have served, and few masters had specialized
tastes in Greek Testaments.

If, in teaching the languages, schoolmasters had to rely on
old textbooks, in arithmetic and mathematical instruction they
could choose among several new ones. At least one, Nicholas Pike's
A New and Complete System of Arithmetic,[12] improved on its
predecessors. Pike's book, ranging over arithmetic, geometry,
algebra, and trigonometry, was especially good in the quality
of its broad coverage. In it problems relating to business appeared just as prominently as in any of the texts used by colonial
masters. As in colonial texts, this practical emphasis cut into
the space which might have been given to the theoretical side

---

9. *Newport Mercury*, June 1, 1789.

10. William Duncan, *Cicero's Select Orations* . . . (London, 1792).

11. The Rev. William Bentley recorded in 1793 that the Preceptor of Dummer
Academy told him that "The teaching by Duncan's Cicero & Davidson's Virgil is so
common . . . that no other School Books are to be found": William Bentley, *Diary of
William Bentley* (4 vols. Salem, Mass., 1905–14), 2, 12.

12. Newburyport, 1788.

of mathematics. Two pages, for example, were devoted to logarithms in Pike; and though their use was described, no explanation of what a logarithm is was offered.

Schoolmasters did not upbraid Nicholas Pike for such omissions; they knew that boys required little theory. Problems which drove home essential mathematical relationships furnished a more valuable lesson. And, as copybooks show, schoolmasters did not hesitate to give their scholars numerous problems to work.[13]

Unsatisfied by simply putting their boys to working problems, careful teachers explained every operation and supervised their scholars' progress. A master in Providence after 1785 could follow suggestions furnished by the school committee on how to teach simple arithmetic—suggestions which were a distillation of the best of contemporary practice. Not surprisingly, the committee's guidance incorporated most standard colonial techniques.

If a master followed the committee's promptings, he proceeded slowly; he moved from the simple to the complex, and he illustrated the rules with problems which his scholars worked. Learning to name and make numbers was the first step, one which boys probably had taken when they entered grammar school. From numeration—the rubric attached to this first step —the master led the way into addition. The wise master kept it "simple" at first, mentioning neither compound numbers nor fractions. Nor did he complicate matters by having his charges add sums of money or weights and measures. When satisfied that his boys could add, the master taught his scholars the "square Multiplication table" in which sums ran from 2 times 1 to 12 times 12. The table was intended to be learned by heart and learn it by heart the scholar did. As memorization without understanding was useless, the master frequently required students to answer questions from the table. This process aided

13. Copybooks in Uncatalogued MSS, Essex Institute, and the Penniman MSS Collection, Yale.

the memory and showed the scholars the value of what they had striven to learn. Subtraction came next. By this time the technique of learning was familiar to the boys. They listened to the explanation and began to work problems. The master pointed out that as subtraction was the reverse of addition "one will serve to prove the other." If he was confident of his scholars' learning at this point, he interjected a number of simple multiplication problems, thereby taxing the boys with two operations at once. This was about as complicated as things became; not until subtraction and multiplication were firmly under control did boys move to division. Division was new to the scholars but the process of teaching was familiar: a simple explanation of rules accompanied by illustrative problems. Once past division, boys could be put to using their elementary skills in solving problems which invoked the Pence Table, Tables of Weights and Measures, the Rule of Reduction, the Rule of Three, and the Rule of Practice. Along with addition, subtraction, multiplication, and division, such problems, masters knew, served as a foundation for higher mathematics, as well as for simple business training.[14]

American-authored textbooks pre-empted the field in mathematics but not in navigation. Here the old guides of the colonial period continued to reign.[15] Yet instruction kept pace with navigational practice—not because of the ingenuity of masters but because practice resisted all change. Unfortunately the old techniques left something to be desired; and New England ships, which were as well handled and as skillfully rigged as any in the world, groped an uncertain way over the seas. Following customary procedures the great ship *Massachusetts* missed its port by more than fifty miles in 1790, an incident

14. Providence, R.I., School Committee, [Minutes of] *A Meeting the 16th of January A.D. 1786* (Providence, 1786).

15. One exception may have been Hartford Grammar, which used John Hamilton Moore, *The Practical Navigator, And Seaman's New Daily Assistant* (4th ed. London, 1774), a book not widely used before the Revolution. See "Rules and Regulations for the Grammar School, Jan. 1790, M. B. Brainerd Collection, Box 114, CHS.

repeated with variations by many other New England vessels.[16]

Finding longitude continued to be the most obstinate problem Yankee navigators faced even though the invention before the Revolution of a chronometer capable of keeping exact time had made a simple and accurate method possible. Astronomers and sailors had hoped for such an instrument since the sixteenth century. They knew that if one were available, longitude could be calculated with ease by making use of certain elementary data. Since at any point on the surface of the earth it is noon when the sun is directly overhead, east of this point it is past noon and west not yet noon. And since the earth rotates fifteen degrees every hour, if the difference in time between some known fixed point and the point where the sun is observed at noon is accurately measured, the position east or west can easily be calculated.[17]

Navigation instructors, even in Salem, do not seem to have explained the importance of the new chronometer.[18] Instead—paralleling seafaring practice—they taught the calculation of longitude from lunar observation and dead reckoning. They also continued to teach boys to find latitude through the use of "double altitudes." [19] Master J. Fraser of Newport, who favored this means, called it the "new method," although it had been known since the sixteenth century and had been standard practice since the seventeenth! [20] No one seems to have claimed that great circle sailing was new, but it and most of the other navigational methods learned by colonial youths held their old places in the post-Revolutionary curriculum.

16. Samuel Eliot Morison, *The Maritime History of Massachusetts* (Boston, 1921), pp. 52, 113–14.

17. Useful studies of the development of navigation are Lawrence C. Wroth, *The Way of a Ship: An Essay on the Literature of Navigation Science* (Portland, Maine, 1937); Samuel Eliot Morison, *Admiral of the Ocean Sea: A Life of Christopher Columbus* (2 vols. Boston, 1942); E. G. R. Taylor, *The Haven-Finding Art* (New York, 1957).

18. I can find nothing resembling such an explanation in the MSS navigation books in the Uncatalogued MSS, Essex Institute.

19. *Providence Gazette*, Oct. 26, 1793.

20. *Newport Mercury*, Nov. 12, 1791.

Surveying had no innovations to resist, and no great new techniques to discover. But as instruments were improved and became cheaper, surveying practice changed and instruction altered. Greater precision became possible, if one could handle the tools of the trade, making imperative the need to get students into the field for on-the-spot instruction. Doing so was not always easy for the master; he, after all, almost always had other students not studying surveying, who could not be left unattended. Yet somehow most masters managed to squeeze in field training to complement classroom work.[21]

Manuals written in New England near the end of the century recognized the trend to field work, and offered suggestions on the conduct of field exercises. Evidence of their use, as of any others, is scanty. The chances are, however, that old books like John Love's continued to enjoy wide popularity.[22]

While mathematics and the learned languages remained comfortably in the colonial rut, rhetoric, attracted by English developments, abandoned the old patch. The change did not come in the forms of instruction; boys in the early Republic spoke pieces (as orations were called) and "pronounced," as boys had done for generations. But with the publication of Hugh Blair's *Lectures on Rhetoric* new rhetorical theory replaced the doctrine of the trope and figure school.[23] Eloquence, Blair defined conventionally, as the "art of persuasion." Persuasion, he said, followed conviction. The distinction between the two was simple: "Conviction affects the understanding only; persuasion the will and practice." [24] The orator's task was to engage his listeners' "affections" in favor of truth. To do this his argument

21. MSS surveying guides in Penniman MSS Collection, Yale, and Uncatalogued MSS, Essex Institute. *Connecticut Gazette*, Apr. 30, 1784. *Conn. Journal*, June 12, 1793.

22. *Geodaesia: or the Art of Surveying* . . . (London, 1771).

23. 2 vols. Philadelphia, 1793. Blair's *Essays on Rhetoric: Abridged Chiefly from Dr. Blair's Lectures on That Science* (Boston, 1789) was probably read more widely in New England. For examples of Blair's popularity see Jeremiah Day to Stephen Twining, Nov. 18, 1795, Jeremiah Day Papers, Yale; Vinson Gould to Thomas Day, Jan. 24, 1795, Thomas Mills Day Papers, Yale.

24. Blair, *Essays*, p. 147.

had to be "solid," his method "clear." "Good sense must be its foundation." [25] These were the most essential requisites if true eloquence was to convince. This suggests that Blair had no use for "art" in rhetoric; he did, but his pronouncements on its behalf were less energetic. Once the orator had convinced his listeners, had won their understandings, he had then to address their passions and move their hearts. Hence, "besides solid argument and clear method, all the captivating and interesting arts, both composition and pronunciation, enter into the idea of eloquence." [26] But these arts must never be substituted for the argument itself.

Dissenters from Blair's rhetorical theory inevitably argued for a more enthusiastic oratory—one which appealed less to the understanding than to the passions. James Burgh's *The Art of Speaking* [27] furnished such advocates of enthusiastic eloquence with a guide which—while it recognized Blair's authority— placed an entirely different emphasis on the techniques and ends of oratory. "True eloquence," Burgh declared, "does not wait for constant *approbation*." Indeed if "it allows *time* to *criticize*, it is not *genuine*." It ravishes the listener's affections, crushes his will until "His *passions* are no longer *his own*. The *orator* has taken *possession* of them; and with superior power, works them to whatever he *pleases*." [28] To achieve such mastery Burgh prescribed a method which stressed form over content. His book indeed did not pretend to deal with substance: Part one was composed of an essay which provided instructions "for expressing properly the principal Passions and Humours, which occur in Reading or public Speaking"; [29] Part two furnished eighty-one selections from classical and modern writers which might be spoken in practicing the rules of the first section.

Instruction in rhetoric did not pause long over the fine

25. Ibid.
26. Ibid.
27. 5th ed. Newburyport, 1782. Timothy Dwight in his academy seems to have used this edition; see Daniel Goodwin to Ebenezer Barnard, July 8, 1791, Goodwin Papers, CHS.
28. Burgh, *Art of Speaking*, p. 42.
29. Ibid., title page.

points of theory. But schoolmasters were aware of the differences, and seem to have taught along the lines prescribed by one theory or another. For boys, theory became important only if it affected the way they were coached to deliver pieces. In some schools, Burgh's guide, or others like it provided the pieces. In others no manual was used and they pronounced their own compositions or their masters'.[30]

When the question "What did you do in school today?" was asked and a colonial lad replied "I recited grammar," everyone knew he meant Latin grammar. After the Revolution, as English grammar appeared in more curricula, this reply would have been ambiguous. As a subject suitable for study by Latin scholars, English grammar had never earned many supporters; but as the craving for utility in education grew, many New Englanders came to believe that it should be taught. Moderns pointed to its various uses; parents who expected tangibles to issue from education, school committees who admired the useful, and boys who dreaded to meet the ablative agreed that it should be given a place in the curriculum, though most did not believe that it should crowd the learned languages out altogether.

The case for English grammar was made more persuasive by those who insisted that an American version should be taught. In his brash way, Noah Webster supplied most of their argument. America, he urged, offered an opportunity to restore a pure English language, in particular the language of the early eighteenth century. English grammar had been corrupted by the foolish attempt to impose Latin rules upon it. The two standard texts of the colonial period—Dilworth's and Lowth's —suffered, according to Webster, from their addiction to Latin forms. Dilworth's he dismissed as "a mere Latin grammar, very indifferently translated." [31] The dictum of the ancients that a

30. Anonymous Diary, Student in Plainfield Academy, M. B. Brainerd Collection. *Newport Mercury,* Feb. 19, Mar. 5, 1787.

31. Noah Webster, *A Grammatical Institute of the English Language* . . . (Hartford, 1784).

knowledge of Latin equipped the scholar to understand English he branded as a "stupid opinion." [32]

His own book lopped off the Latin rubrics which had encumbered other grammars, and attempted to follow usage in establishing its own categories and rules. Verbs, for example, it placed in two categories, transitive and intransitive, insisting that the "common division into *active,* passive and neuter, is very inaccurate. We have no passive verb in the language; and those which are called neuter are mostly active." [33] Though the book could claim some uniqueness in its grammatical approach, it offered only the conventional exercise for students to follow. Writing bad English into good—or "false construction"—and parsing had served in English grammar for years. Parsing, of course, smacked of the detested Latin.

Webster's nationalism converted many, and his system, as his ideas on grammatical construction came to be called, pleased others. Though teaching his system did not call for new methods, masters insisted on devising fresh techniques, especially the coupling of grammar and composition. Boys studying with such teachers, we may be sure, wrote themes, though usually only a day or two in a week was given to such exercises. For example, in Hartford Grammar School in the early 1790s boys studied English grammar two days a week but composed less frequently. Woburn Grammar School, which used two texts, required composition once every two weeks—but only of upper classmen. Boston was no more progressive; there the first and second classes of the Grammar School received daily instruction in English grammar from a writing master, but they do not seem to have written themes every day.[34]

Boys working through Webster's *Grammatical Institute* may have been unaware that they were studying an American version of English. And those who learned geography from Jedidiah

32. Ibid.
33. Ibid., p. 16 n.
34. Hartford Grammar School Records; Woburn Town Records, *12, 75. Massachusetts Centinel,* Jan. 9, 1790.

Morse's text *Geography Made Easy* may not have realized that the book was written by an American.[35] But they could not miss Morse's contention that American geography—not English or European—was the proper study for American boys. For too long a time, Morse insisted, American boys had been educated "rather as the subjects of the British King, than as the citizens of a free republick." [36] Yet his book was neither aggressively republican nor blatantly nationalistic, and it treated the English generously. Morse, in fact, was scarcely able to restrain his admiration for the English, praising everything from their bravery to the beauty of their women. His enthusiasm for them cooled when he discussed the Revolution —but even on this still tender subject he was calm and dispassionate.[37]

Though impartial in tone, the book's emphasis was clearly on the United States. As fair as he was in his judgments of Britain, Morse devoted but few pages to that country. And the rest of the world received even more cursory mention.

Morse judged his audience shrewdly, for within a few years after its publication his geography was the most widely used text in New England. Not surprisingly, schoolmasters employed old methods in teaching it—their scholars read, memorized, and recited. If there was an innovation in teaching geography, it was in the greater use of maps and globes, now available in greater quantities and cheaper too.[38]

Before the Revolution the ordinary girl never dreamed of studying any of these subjects. When the matter of education came up, she was solemnly reminded of her intellectual inferiority and of her obligations to home and family. Reading and

35. *Geography Made Easy. Being a Short but Comprehensive System of That Very Useful and Agreeable Science* (New Haven, 1784).

36. Ibid., p. v.

37. Ibid., pp. 60–61, 184.

38. For the sale of Morse's text see Jedidiah Morse to his father, Jan. 8, 1785, Morse Family Papers, Yale. Among other schools it was used at Woburn and Hartford.

writing, a little arithmetic, and needlework, she was told, constituted the proper training for her.

Although these same subjects continued hardly less important in the new nation, the grounds on which they were recommended shifted. A girl of the young Republic could not always be persuaded by homilies which announced that it was her "duty" to learn the domestic skills. She awaited assurance that a subject was genteel and that it would help make her into an accomplished woman. Such recommendations were often made on behalf of the plainest arts; even housework came disguised as an accomplishment—"an accomplishment to a princess," Simeon Baldwin once assured his niece.[39]

Colonial girls had sometimes heard similar sentiments, for pride in the genteel woman had existed before the Revolution, especially among the upper classes. But it was muted at that time, while in the early days of the Republic it became a part of the idiom of the day. The lady of quality came to furnish the most prominent educational ideal for women.

As in the colonial period she was a romanticized figure, pure in mind and heart and full of charm and refinement. Her accomplishments carefully skirted the traditional male domain of the learned languages, higher mathematics, and natural sciences. Still they were impressive. She could sing and play the pianoforte and dance and sketch a landscape. And although she could not boast a profound knowledge of history or geography or English literature, she at least had sampled those disciplines. For her these were ornamental subjects; they brightened her wit and polished her conversation without demanding much of her intellect. She was, after all, expected to show her familiarity with the world of letters but at the same time to show that she was not of it. As one of the widely read guides to gentility pointed out, "learned lady" was an "epithet" no girl "should ever acquire."[40] Nor should a lady's learning go on parade;

39. Simeon Baldwin to his niece Dolly, Jan. 12, 1784, Baldwin Family Papers, Yale.
40. Enos Hitchcock, *Memoirs of the Bloomsgrove Family* (2 vols. Boston, 1790), 2, 84.

rather it should be covered with "a gentle veil." [41] Even the domestic arts were more important than the higher learning, and the girl who aspired to accomplishment knew that she would have to learn to cook and sew.[42]

Alone, these accomplishments did not confer gentility. They were, for all their importance, external to it. True gentility affected the heart of the girl. She was above all religious—religion, indeed, was the only subject of which she had more than a perfunctory knowledge. Knowing the Bible better than any other book, praying regularly, and living according to Christian principles, she was a model of piety.

The genteel ideal did not imply equality; and a girl was never permitted to forget that she was inferior to men. As in the colonial period, men—and especially the clergy—continued to lay her inferiority at Heaven's door. "While man is called the lord of creation, and has dominion given him over all things," the Reverend John Ogden argued in 1791, "woman taken from his side, bears his image, and is placed as his companion. Their mutual union is descriptive of the union between Christ and his church." [43] Such an explanation was congenial to male vanity and was accordingly repeated often. So also was the view that held women themselves partially responsible for their low position. According to it, women paid inordinate attention to dress and appearance, they courted flattery, they sought pleasure, and they revealed a distressing propensity to shirk work in favor of amusement. Their behavior exposed defects which no amount of polish and no accomplishments could conceal.[44]

41. *Newport Mercury*, Aug. 16, 1787.

42. This paragraph and the next are based on Hitchcock, *Memoirs of the Bloomsgrove Family*; Hannah Foster, *The Boarding School* (Boston, 1898); Hester M. Chapone, *Letters on the Improvement of the Mind* (2d ed. London, 1773); Constantia [Judith Murray] *The Gleaner, A Miscellaneous Production* (3 vols. Boston, 1798); and scattered essays in newspapers and magazines—especially *Massachusetts Centinel*, Apr. 16, 1788; *Newport Mercury*, July 8, 1789; and *Massachusetts Magazine*, Nov. 1792.

43. John Cosens Ogden, *An Address Delivered at the Opening of Portsmouth Academy* (Portsmouth, 1791), p. 16.

44. *Massachusetts Magazine*, Nov. 1792.

Recognition of inherent imperfections did not discourage the pursuit of gentility. Indeed, to satisfy the expectations of parents that female education would provide accomplishments, schoolmistresses devised curricula along genteel lines. One such dame, Miss Sally Pierce of Litchfield, Connecticut, probably pleased parents more than most. Miss Sally, as her girls called her, earned a great reputation as a gentle but firm teacher who combined useful and ornamental learning with extraordinary skill. She deserved the good opinion of parents, for though her girls were burdened with the inevitable sewing, they also received instruction in history, geography, English literature and grammar, French, painting, drawing, and music.[45]

Miss Pierce taught the academic subjects in ways familiar to boys' schools. Her girls learned geography, for example, by working through Guthrie—probably replaced by Morse early in the next century—studying its contents and reciting their store of facts regularly for their teacher. And when they came to English grammar, they parsed just as any boy did.[46]

History, Miss Pierce believed, should be put to some non-historical uses. In her school, as in many others, it drove home a lesson in morality. Reading the history of England, for example, her girls learned to contrast favorably their own happy period of religious toleration with the dark years of persecution under Charles I. In Miss Pierce's hands even Charles Rollins' *The Ancient History of the Egyptians, Carthagenians, Assyrians* became a moral tale; its accounts of kings, courts, and battles were all "improved" to paint the beauty of virtue and the Christian life.[47]

Following Miss Pierce through Rollins was an arduous task, for she raced through a volume in about two weeks. Swift as the pace was, the girls knew that they would have to remember

45. For Miss Pierce's school see the "Diary of Charlotte Sheldon [1796]" in Emily N. Vanderpoel, *Chronicles of a Pioneer School* (Cambridge, Mass., 1903), pp. 10–17; and L. H. Moseley, ed., *The Diaries of Julia Cowles, A Connecticut Record, 1797–1803* (New Haven, 1931).

46. "Diary of Charlotte Sheldon," pp. 12–14.

47. *Diaries of Julia Cowles*, p. 3.

the facts of the story as well as the moral; Miss Pierce, who listened to recitations almost daily, saw to that. Recitations must have been disappointing affairs if she had many students like Julia Cowles. For Julia, who attended the school in the 1790s, often recorded in her diary the sad confession: "I cannot recollect any of the History read this day." [48] Julia, if her diary reflected the state of her knowledge, never quite comprehended Rollins even on days when her memory served her better.

Miss Pierce seems to have attempted to direct her girls to the right kind of literary works, as the genteel ideal enjoined, to those which "convey lessons for moral improvement." This was an injunction easier to state than to carry out, for girls preferred something with a little more spice—novels, for example. But novels, Miss Pierce undoubtedly told her girls, were dangerous because they excited the passions and contained examples of immorality.[49] Yet she permitted her girls to read them because she knew that they also contained good moral examples. How much moral improvement the girls actually derived may be questioned. Charlotte Sheldon, one of Miss Pierce's students, reacted to the Gothic romance *The Recess* not with piety but with a girlish "I wanted to have it end happily." [50]

Charlotte also read Goldsmith's *The Citizen of the World* and his *Animated Nature*, Voltaire's *Nanine*, and several of Shakespeare's plays. This mixture of good literature with bad was not uncommon—the girls apparently enjoying the latter at least as well as the former. But on every list—if it was carefully selected—appeared books designed to improve morals. Charlotte, for example, read Helen Maria Williams' *Letters from France*, Vicesimus Knox's *Essays*, and Watts' *On the Mind*, as well as *Memoirs of the Bloomsgrove Family*, *Charlotte's Letters*, and the *Children's Friend*, among others.[51]

48. Ibid., p. 5. See also pp. 8, 10.

49. Mrs. Bloomsgrove, in Hitchcock's *Memoirs of the Bloomsgrove Family*, 2, 87, praised Richardson's *Clarissa* but deplored its "love scenes, which interest the passions more than the understanding."

50. *Diary of Charlotte Sheldon*, p. 15.

51. Helen Maria Williams, *Letters on the French Revolution, Written in France* . . .

A girl's reading—if she followed the prescription of the genteel ideal—took her into areas uncharted by boys. Charlotte Sheldon, for example, read in Buffon's *Natural History* and Lavater's *Essays on Physiognomy*. But these forays tended to be brief and were soon followed by other literary excursions, no more profoundly pursued. None of her reading, as far as one can tell from her diary, aroused her intellectually, but then, her intellect was never engaged.[52]

Her reading, unfortunately, was like her total education, carried on sporadically, sometimes aimlessly, and scarcely ever intensively. Because they were rarely encouraged to probe deeply, girls failed to be sharply altered by their reading. This was appropriate to the genteel ideal, which, after all, advised educational exposure with the sole expectation that the surface would be more highly polished. A girl's substance, if safely Christian, needed no reshaping.

(Boston, 1791) and *Letters from France: Containing Many New Anecdotes Relative to the French Revolution and the Present State of French Manners* (Boston, 1792). Vicesimus Knox, *Essays, Moral and Literary* (London, 1741). W. James, *The Letters of Charlotte, during Her Connexion with Werther* (Dublin, 1786). Arnaud Berguin, *The Children's Friend, and Youth's Monitor* (New Haven, 1798 and earlier editions).

52. There were many editions of Buffon. J. C. Lavater, *Essays on Physiognomy for the Promotion of the Knowledge and the Love of Mankind* (Boston, 1790).

PART III

THE FRUIT OF THE TRADITION, 1700–1800

12. Masters and Scholars

FEW schools could claim a master like the one in Goldsmith's *Deserted Village* who filled the admiring rustics with wonder "That one small head could carry all he knew." The exceptions stood out: Boston, for example, regarded Ezekiel Cheever with awe during the thirty-eight years he instructed there. Cheever even earned the love and respect of Cotton Mather, who respected few men and loved fewer still. But as a founder of New Haven Colony and a master who had taught grammar schools in Ipswich and Charlestown before coming to Boston, Cheever appeared a patriarch when he arrived in 1670.[1]

Unlike Cheever, the typical master had no intention of remaining in the classroom for more than a year or two. In most cases he had just been graduated from Harvard or Yale and was teaching because he did not know what else to do while weighing his opportunities; or, more often perhaps, the school was simply a means to keep himself alive while studying law, medicine, or theology or looking for an opening in business. At the same time, like Archibald Hall of a Norwich, Connecticut, school, he may have looked upon the young ladies in his school with hopes that had nothing to do with a career. Hall, plainly a fancier of pretty girls, confessed in 1785 that "I have some prospects of Laying-foundation for future happiness in town by selecting from my school a lovely sweetheart."[2]

1. For Cotton Mather on Cheever see *Corderius Americanus* (Boston, 1708).
2. Archibald Hall to Simeon Baldwin, Sept. 26, 1785, Baldwin Family Papers, Yale. The first part of this paragraph is based on teachers' letters, especially those in the Robert Treat Paine Papers, MHS; the Baldwin Family Papers; and the sketches in Shipton, *Biographical Sketches*, and Dexter, *Biographical Sketches of the Graduates of Yale*.

A young man nearing graduation, or recently graduated, was in a good position, for school committees seeking teachers naturally turned to the colleges. There they could find young men who knew the languages, mathematics and some science, and about whose morals anxious parents might be assured by the testimony of the college authorities. When approached, the colleges did their best for their sons, especially where salary was concerned. In the early winter of 1783, for example, Colonel Labdiah Rogers wrote President Ezra Stiles of Yale on behalf of a Norwich school committee asking him to recommend an instructor for the town's new academy.[3] Stiles favored Samuel Austin but turned over the business of writing a letter of recommendation to Tutor Simeon Baldwin. From Baldwin's pen came a shrewdly worded letter which aimed not simply at persuading the Norwich committee to hire Austin but to hire him at a handsome salary. Austin he described as "one of the first Scholars of his class in scientific Literature, & knowledge in general—of a pious character & much steadiness—joined with graceful Manners & an engaging behavior."[4] Austin was, in short, just the sort of "character which you want." The catch was that Austin was teaching in New Haven, where according to Baldwin he received "about 115£" a year, and where he was "dear to the People." The implication was plain enough: the popular Austin was not to be drawn from New Haven cheaply. To make certain that the committee did not miss the point, Baldwin urged that it offer a greater wage than £115 a year, and told the Norwich group that "Such a Character as you need, could not be obtained for the scanty pittance of a common Schoolmasters Sallery." The committee was impressed and Austin got the job, though he may have settled for less than £115. Yet the initial Norwich offer was high enough—$400 a year.[5]

Indeed had the amount of Austin's salary been known to

3. Simeon Baldwin to Labdiah Rogers, Dec. 8, 1783, Baldwin Family Papers.
4. Ibid., Dec. 8, 1783.
5. Jacob Witter to Simeon Baldwin, Jan. 20, 1784, Baldwin Family Papers.

other schoolmasters he would have been a much envied man, for keeping school was not the way to wealth. On the other hand, teachers' pay was not as low as it is commonly pictured. And during the eighteenth century it increased—in some cases fairly rapidly.

At the opening of the century the average yearly salary paid a village schoolmaster was about £30.[6] Watertown's masters netted this sum until 1715, when the town raised the stipend to £36. Thereafter, salaries gradually increased to £40 in 1717, £44 in 1722, £45 in 1727, £55 in 1733, £90 old tenor in 1745, £100 old tenor in 1746, £165 old tenor in 1748, £250 old tenor in 1749, and £300 old tenor in 1750. In 1748 the Watertown master also received his board, but during the next two years he boarded himself. The salary at Watertown and the rate of increases seem to have been representative of village pay all over New England. In the 1760s the average salary at Watertown was £65, which was increased to £75 in 1775. Increases continued after the Revolution, until near the end of the century the average salary outside the cities was about £100.[7]

The size of a town, its location, the number of scholars, and other local conditions largely determined the salary it had to pay to attract a master. Small isolated towns usually had the most difficulty hiring masters, for most Harvard and Yale graduates looked down on small villages, liked to be near either their college or home, and preferred teaching grammar scholars to abecedarians. A number of these desires influenced Robert Treat Paine when, after graduating from Harvard in 1749, he accepted a schoolmaster's place in Lunenburg. A few months later he began searching for a school closer to Boston. Offered a better salary in Bristol, he refused—probably because of that town's distance from home. Finally, in 1750, he gave up his school and became usher at Boston Latin, which probably carried less pay and authority than his position in Lunenburg but

6. I have arrived at this sum after study of town records and letters cited throughout.

7. Watertown Records, 2, 231, 246, 300, 336; 3, 82, 295; 5, 2, 41, 54, 78.

which offered life in the city.[8] In the case of Nathan Prince in Plymouth in 1719, pay and comfortable living outweighed an opportunity to teach in Dorchester, which was closer to Boston. At Plymouth he netted £50 a year and was furnished wood, candles, and a chamber. His board was seven shillings a week. Dorchester offered almost as much money, £49 instead of £50, but the town did not furnish wood and candles. Scholars were more numerous there too, and the more scholars, the more work for the master.[9]

The amount collected by the man who set up for himself depended on the number of students he attracted. Throughout the colonial period the going rate rarely seems to have exceeded a shilling a week per student, but after the Revolution it increased slightly. A few schoolmasters, like Solomon Blakeslee in East Haddam, who reported in 1794 that he had only three students, gave up their school for lack of students.[10] But others, like Samuel Stebbins of Rockyhill, who urged a parent to move his son to another school because he had too many scholars, were overrun by students and doubtless did well financially.[11]

For the schoolmaster the important question about pay was "will it support me?" Most teachers, young and unmarried, probably found the answer to be "yes—quite easily." Simeon Baldwin, who kept a school in New Haven in 1781–82 while he was at Yale, discovered this to be true even though as a graduate student he had to meet extra expenses. Between October 27, 1781, and August 1, 1782, he collected £81 10s. 9d. in salary and spent during the same period (actually from October 12, 1781, to August 1, 1782—two weeks longer) the sum of £60 17s. 4d. He owed and paid later in August 1782 tuition charges of £7 17s. 4d., and £4 4s. for board covering the period

8. For Paine at Lunenburg see Samuel Haven to Robert Treat Paine, Sept. 25, 1749; Abigail Paine to Paine, Oct. 4, 1749. For the Bristol offer see Jeremiah Finney to Paine, Mar. 26, 1750; and Joseph Greenleaf to Paine, Mar. 13, 1749/50. For Paine in Boston see William Downe to Paine, June 18, 1750, Robert Treat Paine Papers.

9. Nathan Prince to Thomas Prince, Oct. 30, 1719, Miscellaneous MSS, Bound, MHS.

10. Solomon Blakeslee to Noah Scovell, Oct. 20, 1794, Scovell Papers, CSL.

11. Samuel Stebbins to Noah Scovell, Apr. 4, 1792, Scovell Papers.

from the middle of June to the end of August. Even with the charges for tuition and other college expenses (which most masters did not have to meet), he managed to live without denying himself much. He went to a ball (12s. 2d.), bought six of Joel Barlow's poems (5s.), two books (12s. 8d.), and a pamphlet (2s. 6d.); supplied himself with the necessities of life; and managed to contribute a shilling "to God" besides. Altogether for this period he came out with a surplus of a little more than £7.[12]

Pay was only one concern of the schoolmaster. Keeping school did not absorb all his energies nor satisfy all his needs. His social and intellectual life—not a problem at college—sometimes suffered in small isolated towns. Young graduates away from sophisticated Cambridge and New Haven often found the country folk dull. "I am here (in eximo subobscura)," Israel Cheever wrote from Wrenthan in 1749, "[where I] have not the fashionable People of the world to converse with." [13] To make matters worse, his lodgings and the countryside furnished unwanted company: there were no bedbugs, he rejoiced, but "theres Chipping squirrels moscatoes, bats, and Night Hawks enough to make it up." [14]

Like Cheever, many masters missed college and the friends made there. Eager for news, they conducted a lively correspondence. They gossiped about jobs and pay, about students and discipline, and, of course, about girls. They commented on careers and prospects; they gave one another advice on how to handle students and parents. And when spicier subjects lacked, they sometimes even exchanged problems in arithmetic. No morsel was too small for youths starved for conversations with their own kind.[15]

Those who studied law or theology, or who read as exten-

12. Simeon Baldwin Account Book, Baldwin Family Papers.
13. Israel Cheever to Robert Treat Paine, July 27, 1749, Robert Treat Paine Papers.
14. Ibid.
15. See the Robert Treat Paine Papers and the Baldwin Family Papers.

sively as Thomas Robbins did, probably repined less than others.[16] Certainly this was true of Stanley Griswold of Norwich, Connecticut, who spent his leisure reading history and studying Hebrew. One evening a week he also attended the meeting of a literary society, where he could talk with other recent graduates of Yale.[17] Timothy Langdon, who confessed "I study none," did not seek intellectual companionship in Farmington, Connecticut, but he, like Archibald Hall, enjoyed female company and the social life of his town.[18]

Hall and Langdon were happy as teachers, and so were many others. Most masters considered their work useful, and many spent hours outside the classroom correcting papers and preparing exercises for their charges. Yet almost all gave up teaching a few years after they started, entering business or the professions. Their motives in leaving teaching were mixed, but most were looking for money. Business, medicine, and law—all could be made to pay more than teaching and held possibilities of great wealth for some. Even the ministry, which held out only minimal financial attractions, usually paid more than teaching.

Since wealth helped determine social status, denying high pay to schoolmasters amounted to refusing them high social position. A schoolmaster ranked above laborers and some men in the middle class, but he knew that in another field his education might gain him much greater recognition. The community in fact expected more of its college graduates than a career in a schoolhouse. This was increasingly true later in the eighteenth century. For as time passed, the schoolmaster's status declined—not because his salary declined (it did not, as we have seen), but because as commercial society in New England grew, so also did the number and variety of careers open to young men. The

16. Increase N. Tarbox, ed., *Diary of Thomas Robbins, D.D., 1796–1854* (2 vols. Boston, 1886), I, 49–54.

17. Stanley Griswold to Simeon Baldwin, Dec. 23, 1786, Baldwin Family Papers.

18. Timothy Langdon to Simeon Baldwin, Dec. 1781, Baldwin Family Papers.

increase inevitably diminished the standing of teaching—a career that could offer little by way of new opportunity.[19]

The boys the masters faced in the classroom differed widely in social backgrounds. Evidence is scanty as to who studied the classics, but we do know that every college student received instruction in the languages before matriculating as a freshman. Analysis of the biographies of Harvard graduates between 1700 and 1739 reveals that the sons of ministers, merchants, wealthy farmers, and high provincial officials consistently made up between 35 and 45 per cent of the student body. At the opposite end of the social scale, shopkeepers, small farmers, and artisans fathered about 30 per cent of Harvard's graduates. The smallest group of students, about 15 per cent, came from the families of lower officials and professionals—a group containing some wealthy men but many more of moderate means. The social status of the remaining students cannot be determined, but most were probably of humble origin.[20]

Boys of all backgrounds understandably looked at school differently from their masters. They sometimes complained about their instructors and often about the difficulty of schoolwork, but most of the time they found life pleasant. This was especially true of scholars attending boarding schools, where, free of parental scrutiny, they found undreamed of opportunities for misbehavior. Making the most of these opportunities entailed evasion of rules, which sometimes could be irritatingly comprehensive. At Plainfield Academy, for example, scholars could not enter taverns, buy on credit, go hunting or riding, or even change boarding houses without permission from their parents or the rector. If a student was found guilty of "im-

19. The brother and sister of Thomas Robbins considered his taking a school after preaching "rather descending": Ammi Robbins to Thomas Robbins, Jan. 10, 1800, Thomas Robbins Correspondence, Box 361, CHS.

20. I have relied on Shipton (Vols. 4–10) for this information. In the years 1700–39, there were slightly more than 1,000 graduates.

moral, indecent or profane language, or improper conduct," he
could expect to be "exemplarily punished." [21] (If this list of
prohibitions was constructed from a record of misdemeanors,
Plainfield must have been a lively place.) On Sundays boys had
to tread softly: they were required to go to church and were
not permitted to do anything else.[22]

If Daniel Goodwin's life at the Academy was typical, the
rules did not cramp the ordinary scholar's style. Daniel, the
ward of Ebenezer Barnard, a substantial Hartford merchant,
arrived in the summer of 1790. He liked the place immediately,
declaring soon after his arrival that he was as content there as
at home. And little wonder! Though he boarded with John
Douglass, one of the proprietors of the Academy and a prominent citizen of Plainfield, he was practically on his own outside
the classroom. His guardian, disapproving of such freedom, re-
quested Douglass to keep the lad busy after school hours. An
impossible task, Douglass replied, for the example of two other
boys boarding with him who were free of his restraint under-
mined his authority with Daniel.[23]

From Plainfield Daniel moved to Timothy Dwight's Greenfield Academy and a year later to Southington for study with
a private master. Though he did not commit serious mischief
at either place, he sometimes tried his guardian's patience. He
spent too much money, he neglected writing home, he shirked
his studies, and he displayed an unhealthy interest in lotteries—
once going so far as to request Barnard to buy a chance in one
in his name. This last crime brought a mild rebuke and a
suggestion that he subscribe to a fund for the Hartford Court
House instead. Barnard, it seems, considered lotteries as a "Spe-
cies of gambling." [24] Though Daniel frequently promised reform, none of his lapses troubled him greatly. The only event

21. Larned, *History of Windham County*, 2, 321.

22. Ibid.

23. Daniel Goodwin to Captain Ebenezer Barnard, Jr., July 10, 1790. J. Douglass to
Ebenezer Barnard, Aug. 2, 1790, Goodwin Papers, CHS.

24. Ebenezer Barnard to Daniel Goodwin, Sept. 2, 1793, Goodwin Papers.

which managed to damp his lightheartedness was "the itch," which he got four times in less than a year at Southington. With the fourth infection he decided he preferred home to school and appealed for immediate release.[25]

Most of Daniel's misdeeds occurred outside the classroom and riled his guardian more than his instructors. Other boys chose the school for their bad conduct. Though conventional accounts of eighteenth-century education describe the master keeping his students in hand through a liberal use of the birch, the reactions of masters varied considerably. Masters fond of the rod existed, but most seem to have preferred to use other means. Some, hardly more than boys themselves, had trouble keeping their charges in hand.[26] The unhappy Simeon Breed complained in 1782 that he was "continually harassed with 'Master m'I go out [and] Master m'I go to the Fire.' "[27] By the following year he was so desperate that he avoided everyone outside of his classroom. Timothy Langdon, on the other hand, handled the Farmington school with pleasure and exuberance. To Simeon Baldwin—also teaching in 1781—he described their situations as that of absolute rulers: "you & I are both Presidents—Ay & more than that we are Kings (if not tyrants) we issue law and govern our little societies as we please. . . . In short we are Judge, Jury & executioner."[28] Although Thomas Robbins took life and himself much more seriously ("May I do some good") than Langdon did, he enjoyed teaching and at Torringford did not find it necessary to scold even one of his students, though they were all boys from fourteen to eighteen years of age.[29] If

---

25. Daniel's request for a lottery ticket is in his letter to Barnard, Aug. 26, 1793. For his appeals for money see Goodwin to Barnard, July 20, 1791; his admission of extravagance with a bill for it, Goodwin to Barnard, Feb. 10, 1792; Barnard complains of Daniel's failure to write home in Barnard to Goodwin, Dec. 1, 1791; his account of the itch, Goodwin to Barnard, Mar. 1793 (endorsed as received 12 Mar.), Goodwin Papers.

26. Daniel Crocker to Simeon Baldwin, Nov. 1782, Baldwin Family Papers.

27. Simeon Breed to Simeon Baldwin, Apr. 2, 1782; see also Breed to Baldwin, Nov. 1783: Baldwin Family Papers.

28. Timothy Langdon to Simeon Baldwin, Dec. 1781, Baldwin Family Papers.

29. Tarbox, *Diary of Thomas Robbins*, 1, 53–54.

things really got out of hand, parents could always be appealed to and probably were informed of their boys' more serious misdemeanors. Captain Noah Scovell was told of his son's skipping out just before an examination at Cheshire Academy and was warned by the school's head that "in [the] future . . . I shall Look for an intire Submission to all its [the Academy's] Rules & Injunctions." [30] A few months later Scovell's other son at the Academy apparently committed a lesser breach, but his father learned of it only when he received the Academy's financial account which billed him for a pane of glass and lock broken by his son. [31]

Parents did not always side with the schoolmaster. Eli Whitney, teaching in Hopkinston, made the mistake of whipping a boy whose father enjoyed litigation. Two days after the chastisement Whitney found himself in court facing a charge of assault and battery. His own father settled with the testy parent out of court. From that time on, Whitney seems to have favored persuasion over the birch. [32]

Girls were probably less troublesome to their teachers. Jedidiah Morse, who had as many as sixty girls in his school in 1785, often commented on how "agreeable" the school was to him. [33] On the day that he closed it after several successful years, a scene "sufficient to melt the hardest heart" took place. The girls —"delicate, pretty young Misses"—were "all in tears" and the tender-hearted Morse probably was not far from them himself. "I loved them," he declared not long afterwards, "& I think I may assuredly say they in general esteemed their Instructor— very happy am I in the reflection." [34]

Although diverting, misbehavior did not supply all the recreation a boy desired. If he lived at home he could, of course, take part in the social affairs open to adolescents in his town.

30. John Bowden to Noah Scovell, Mar. 23, 1799, Scovell Papers.

31. "Account rendered to Capt. Scovell, July 5, 1799," Scovell Papers.

32. Diary, entries for Dec. 16, 17, 18, 19, 1788; Eli Whitney Papers, Yale.

33. Jedidiah Morse to his father, Oct. 29, 1783, Apr. 20, 27, May 23, 1785, Morse Family Papers, Yale.

34. Ibid., Sept. 13, 1785.

In most large towns and many villages there were dancing schools which boys could resort to, and singing schools, especially after the Revolution, were also popular.[35]

A lad in a boarding school might find entertainment scarce, for such schools rarely sponsored much recreation. One that did, Sharon Academy, Connecticut, seems to have been an exception. Dances were held in the academy once a month in the 1790s, sometimes wild affairs with much drinking. On one occasion town boys—"ruffian fellows" according to a Sharon scholar—invaded the ball. A fight ensued which the Academy boys won, but not before the interlopers had the satisfaction of giving one of the scholars a black eye.[36]

Sharon scholars really did not need organized recreation, for left to their own devices they managed very nicely. Near at hand were girls who attended the academy and who boarded, as did the boys, with Sharon families. Some of the girls, as the letters of the boys make plain, were lovely, while others were both lovely and of doubtful virtue. Since many of the boys seem to have been unencumbered with conventional moral standards, unorganized recreation at Sharon far surpassed the organized in popularity.[37]

Schoolboys also fished whenever they got the chance and, judging from the drawings in copybooks, dwelt on the pleasures of fishing when they were not actually doing it. In the winter, with streams and ponds frozen over, skating entertained many.

35. For dancing schools see *Columbian Centinel*, Oct. 3, 1792. *Essex Gazette*, Feb. 4, 1772. *Connecticut Courant*, June 4, 1798. Jedidiah Morse taught a singing school in Guilford, Conn., in 1783, and commented on how popular such schools were in a letter to his father, Mar. 19, 1783, Morse Family Papers. See also *Connecticut Courant*, June 4, 1798, for an example of an advertisement for such a school. The newspapers contain many examples.

36. For the fight see Vinson Gould to Thomas Mills Day, Sept. 29, 1793. See also Sally Downs to Thomas Mills Day, Jan. 2, 1794; Abijah Holcomb to Thomas Mills Day, Apr. 10, 1794; Vinson Gould to Thomas Mills Day, Feb. 22, 1795: Thomas Mills Day Papers, Yale.

37. Samuel Starr to Thomas Mills Day, July 25, 1793; Nathaniel Holly to Thomas Mills Day, Aug. 15, 1793; Samuel Starr to Thomas Mills Day, Oct. 25, 1793; and other letters in the Thomas Mills Day Papers.

Aside from their regular textbooks boys do not seem to have read much. Of the literature supplied them by parents much was pious stuff—not likely to be considered recreational by the ordinary lad.[38]

Although most of the fun of going to school was enjoyed outside its walls, at least once a year master and scholars joined forces to please themselves and the surrounding community with an exhibition. Especially popular after the Revolution, exhibitions were programs featuring much oratory, dialogues, plays, and singing. The charm of the exhibition derived from the fact that it permitted everyone to participate. Even the trustees, if the school was blessed with such a group, might take part —either in public examination of the boys, which sometimes preceded the main program, or in the speech-making. The master, too, might speak, perhaps even end the evening, as Thomas Robbins once did in Torringford, with an oration.[39]

As important a role as the trustees and master might play, the main part of the exhibition was the performance of the scholars. Most took part in the dialogues or recited other "pieces." The subjects of these efforts varied, but usually they dealt with some moral or patriotic theme. Or they might touch matters close to the hearts of trustees, as did one in Plainfield Academy which "celebrated the promoters of literature universally," and in particular Isaac Coit who had "made a handsome donation" to the school.[40] After the oratory everybody welcomed the singing. Here again the students held the center of the stage, though at Timothy Dwight's Greenfield Academy they sang their master's compositions.[41]

Exhibitions were about the only frills offered by the schools. It is doubtful if they had much value for the student, but they did keep the schools in the public eye and they gave parents

38. For a gift of devotional literature see Anna Goodwin to Daniel Goodwin, Oct. 19, 1792, Goodwin Papers.

39. Tarbox, *Diary of Thomas Robbins*, 1, 53.

40. *Connecticut Gazette*, Mar. 20, 1789.

41. Timothy Dwight to Noah Webster, June 6, 1788, MS in Yale.

an opportunity to get a close look at the master and to test his mettle. That this was not an accurate index to either the master's ability or the quality of his instruction did not prevent him from anxiously preparing his charges and nervously regarding their performance.

No doubt parents usually found these spectacles reassuring. "Our sons are learning," was the delighted reaction of many. And most of the time they were justified in this conclusion, even if they forgot that a lazy or dull boy appeared more diligent and brighter than he really was after his master had carefully rehearsed his performance.

What no one could predict, or even perceive, was that education sometimes produced unexpected, and occasionally even unwelcomed, results.

13. Education as an Intellectual Force

IN 1793 seventeen-year-old Amos Eaton began to prepare for
college. Not content with exercising the boy in the ordinary
grammatical tasks, his master, the Reverend David Porter of
Spencertown, gave him some provocative advice: "Learn the
reason why a thing is so." [1] Eaton apparently took this counsel
seriously and two years later, incited by some "Observations"
in Watts' *Logic,* began questioning "the proofs of Divine revelation," a process which for a time proved disastrous for his
religious convictions.[2]

Brief as it was, Eaton's experience confirms what men in
almost every age suspect—education can be subversive. The
Reverend Porter, of course, did not suppose that his advice
would be employed to dissolve faith. Nor did Isaac Watts, author of hymns and homilies, intend that his *Logic* implant anything but trust in the Christian story.[3]

Their complacency is not surprising, for Eaton's case was
unusual. Only rarely in a boy's education was he obliged to
confront faith with reason; and when he did, faith usually
emerged intact. Yet if the liberal education dispensed in grammar schools and academies did not produce psychic convulsions
in the average boy, it did underscore the growing secularism and
"reasonableness" of the age. By itself liberal education did not
produce a new frame of mind in New England, but it did rein-
force tendencies already present—a concern for this world, religious apathy, and especially the rational strain within Puritanism.

1. Amos Eaton, Journal, Oct. 22, 1793, CHS.
2. Ibid. [no month given], 1795.
3. For a discussion of Watts' *Logic* see above, Chap. 5.

Long before the seventeenth century, men had given a variety of definitions to reason. Two appealed to Puritans. With scholastics and Aristotelians, they held that reason is a faculty which could be employed to extract truth from the external world. In this view, reason did not nourish itself but rather relied on the senses to supply evidence which could be refined into truth. A second conception—which Puritans shared with Augustine and Platonists—described reason itself as the source of truth, a repository of ideas implanted in man at the creation. Weakened by the fall of man, reason in either conception could be rejuvenated by the working of God's grace.[4]

Whatever its character, Puritans were convinced that reason could not disclose the ways of salvation. For God's ideas about saving man did not exist in reason or nature. He had in fact fashioned them after creating the world, and chose to reveal them only through the art of divinity, which, of course, took its inspiration and substance from the Bible. Puritans were certain that reason contained no inherent challenge to the Scriptures. Creator of both, God would not permit conflict between them.[5]

This convenient assumption strengthened the Puritans' tendency to refer most matters to reason. Not that the Scriptures were neglected—they furnished an unchallengeable standard—but Puritans were rarely content to prove a matter from them. They also had to adduce its rationality, emphasizing all the while the harmony of reason and revelation. Thus they took pains to show that ethics, a subject amply treated in the Bible, contained only rational precepts. The moral law was, of course, above reason; God proclaimed it so. Yet the truths of the moral law were true not simply because God made them but also because reason declared them true. Since God was responsible for this harmony, Puritans urged the rationality of ethics, knowing that in so doing they in no way diminished His authority.[6]

While they were proving the truth of propositions by testing

4. Miller, *New England Mind: The Seventeenth Century*, pp. 190–95.
5. Ibid., pp. 188, 194–95.
6. Ibid., pp. 196–99.

them rationally, the Puritans customarily referred to reason as a faculty. In the eighteenth century this practice continued, but at the same time reason took on broader and less precise meanings. It was no longer simply a means of acquiring truth, it was not inquiry or method; it was instead—as it had been for Platonists and Augustinians—a source of ideas. Sometimes, reason was taken to be the ideas themselves, and the ideas usually were considered to be self-evident.

Imprecise conceptions are usually capable of great extension. Eighteenth-century New Englanders realized this and put reason to fresh, and dangerous, uses—some even going so far as to demonstrate the truths of religion by reason. Many such men did not deny the truth of revelation; but instead of positing revelation as the basis of truth, they began with reason and cited revelation as further evidence. Arminians, for example, held that reason alone could prove the existence of God, could establish the morality necessary to good men, and, if it could not establish the doctrine of immortality, could at least demolish the objections to it. Reason had thus become for some a nearly infallible standard.[7]

A scholar could not avoid the rationalism inherent in his education, if by rationalism we mean the belief in man's capacity to use his mind to organize and measure his behavior. He met it first in *The Shorter Catechism*. "What is the chief end of man?" its opening question asked; and though the focus then shifted to God, the *Catechism* remained profoundly concerned with man. The God of *The Shorter Catechism* was an aloof God —his attributes were noted but they did not bring him closer to man. His limitless power was acknowledged, as were his wisdom and mercy. But it was man's relationship to God, the means of conversion accessible to man, man's behavior, and man's obligations to his fellows and to God that were the center of concern.[8]

7. Conrad Wright, *The Beginnings of Unitarianism in America* (Boston, 1955), pp. 135, 142–44, and passim.

Other catechisms concentrated on the role of the spirit, or of Christ, or of the church. Many explicated theology, or made the exposition of the Ten Commandments a vehicle for doctrine. *The Shorter Catechism*, on the other hand, ignored doctrine almost entirely and treated the Commandments moralistically. Its tone was didactic, not emotional; but its aim was not simply to instruct but to convert. The faithful probably did not find it very nourishing, but its appeal to those still outside the church was great.[9]

What meaning scholars and their masters extracted from the Catechism cannot be known, but the chances are that its rational emphasis impressed their minds deeply. For its tone and stress blended with the cast of thought they met in the classics. Most of the works they read were concerned with man, especially with his nature, with his relations to his fellows, and with his reason. Most—like the Protestantism relayed in the Catechism and in the churches of New England—admitted his imperfections but insisted that man had reason and could use it for ordering his life.

Virgil and Cicero, the authors most often studied by New England boys, are cases in point. Both were moralists and both were this-worldly. To be sure, the *Aeneid* did not openly pronounce on the conduct of life and it contained no rules of behavior, but implicit in it was an unshrinking acceptance of the world as it is. In its central figure, Aeneas, Virgil created a character in the great tradition of Rome. A soldier, Aeneas shared some of the weaknesses of the warrior-class, yet he was more than a soldier, he was a founder of a people, a people who were to become Romans. The *Aeneid* was clearly intended to evoke pride in his achievements; Romans, it seemed to say, have

8. I have studied the catechisms in Thomas F. Torrance, ed., *The School Faith: The Catechisms of the Reformed Church* (New York, 1959). I have also relied on the introduction of this admirable book.

9. Ibid., pp. xviii, 261–62.

cause to praise their past and—more—to hope for the future.

Perhaps most boys, charmed by the exotic cast of the *Aeneid*, failed to sense this. If so, in Cicero's *De officiis* they were exposed to an undisguised moral attitude, and one free of diverting scenes of gods and battles. Cicero was here concerned with the duties which "look to the regulation of everyday life." [10] His moral position was flexible—he conceded, and berated the Stoics for not admitting that there are degrees of right and wrong. He invoked no divine standard by which to measure behavior; man had it in his own power to determine what was good and evil in the conduct of life. To be sure, man was a creature of limited understanding, but nonetheless superior to the animals because of his reason. Reason enabled him to comprehend cause and effect; in short, it made him responsible. [11]

Men acting reasonably consult nature to determine what is virtuous and find that behavior in "harmony with Nature" is good. But "the faithful observance of her laws" does not come naturally to man; his appetite sometimes impels him into evil. His greatest resource in countering the pull of appetite is, of course, his reason, which must discipline the will. Moral action follows when "reason commands, [and] appetite obeys." [12]

If Cicero's procedural prescriptions, which assigned a determinative role to reason, recommended his moral views to New Englanders, so also did his activism. Men, he insisted, must act. Not that the pursuit of truth, the life of the mind, was unimportant; indeed seeking truth was natural to man. But unfortunately, men engaged in the search were likely to fall into error; they might assume that the unknown was known and they might squander their energies in "deep study" of obscure and useless matters. To avoid the first, he suggested a careful weighing of the evidence; to avoid the latter he proposed the active life, for "the whole glory of virtue is in activity." [13]

10. Cicero, *De officiis* (Loeb Classical Library, London, 1928), p. 9 (1.7).
11. Ibid., p. 13 (1.11).
12. All quotations are from ibid., p. 103 (1.100–01).
13. Ibid., p. 21 (1.18–19).

There was rigor in Cicero's imperatives, a rigor fully resonant with both the old ascetic convictions and the newer demands of the Protestant ethic. Sensual pleasure, for example, he dismissed as "quite unworthy of the dignity of man." In ordering one's physical needs, the requirements of "health and strength" had to be consulted, not the urges of pleasure. "And if we will only bear in mind the superiority and dignity of our nature, we shall realize how wrong it is to abandon ourselves to excess and to live in luxury and voluptuousness, and how right it is to live in thrift, self-denial, simplicity, and sobriety." [14]

There was much in the classics which was not so congenial to the New England mind—particularly sexual freedom. Though New Englanders were not embarrassed by frankness about sex, they disapproved of licentiousness. Yet they insisted that licentiousness could not be made an excuse for suppressing books. Accordingly parents and masters continued to require their sons to read the classics, hoping that they would appropriate the good and ignore the bad. In this spirit William Ellery wrote approvingly to his grandson of "Horace, whom you are . . . now studying, and who though justly reprehensible for his obscenities, hath liberally disseminated [the] . . . most excellent maxims, and rules of life." [15]

The extent to which classical rationalism and morality penetrated the minds of boys can only be surmised from tantalizing hints in diaries and letters. But one way in which boys were affected by what they read is clear. They picked up a vocabulary, a terminology, which they sometimes used to cope with everyday experience. An admired leader became a Cato, an enemy a Cataline, a skilled farmer an American Cincinnatus. On another level classical education seems to have confirmed the sense of status that scholars acquired in school. This sense was often erroneously high perhaps. Boys with a classical training described themselves as men of learning; they had knowledge

---

14. All quotations are from ibid., p. 103 (1.100–01).

15. William Ellery to William Ellery Channing, Apr. 22, 1795, William Ellery Letters, Newport Historical Society.

denied to lesser mortals; they were men of taste and elegance. Some—even among those who affected genteel ideals—also acquired a genuine respect for learning for its own sake.[16] And for a few like John Adams and his cousin Samuel and his enemy Thomas Hutchinson, the classics furnished a habit of mind about politics and society. They were exceptional men, of course, and their study of the classics continued long after they left school.[17]

Like most New Englanders John and Samuel Adams looked to the classics for the confirmation of old ideas as well as the stimulation of new. For like most men who received liberal educations, they seemed to find classical rationalism reassuring. Reassurance of course came out of the reading they gave the classics; and controlling their reading were rational forces deep and pervasive in the culture of New England. So prepared, the New England mind almost inevitably appropriated the rationalism of the classics.

As long as it could be made to serve modernity, the traditional learning survived. Pronounced useless, even dead, by critics at the time of the American Revolution, classical education continued to find a place for years after in the grammar schools —and most significantly in the academy, the one fresh educational institution of the eighteenth century. But survival exacted a price—an alteration of the old tradition, especially at the calls of commerce and science which demanded that higher mathematics and vocational subjects be taught.

When the eighteenth century opened, these subjects were not an important part of New England education. Their development, their encroachment upon the traditional offerings of the

16. See, for example, Dick Hayden to George Hayden, Jan. 15, 1794, Noah Scovell Papers, CSL.

17. The importance of the classics for colonial political thought has been emphasized many times. Usually the emphasis is on classical ideas of structure, especially the ideas of mixed government and "balance." Cicero's contention that the state was created to protect the individual's property also deserves attention. See *De officiis*, pp. 249, 255 (II.73, 78).

schools, came at the prompting of various private groups, which became in effect a new authority in education challenging at times the authority of the educational tradition established by the Puritans.

But though these bodies altered the liberal tradition in education, they did not usually suggest that it be abandoned; rather they proceeded to add new subjects to the classical curriculum. Change came through accretion, not through repudiation of the old.

Thus at the end of the century if the power of the old tradition was impaired, it was far from extinct. If it had suffered great loss with the decline of the grammar school, it had recovered through the agency of the academy, which taught old subjects as well as new.

This persistence of liberal education suggests that New Englanders were reluctant to discard the familiar so long as they could convert it to the useful, a process made easier by the long-standing Puritan insistence that the classics had utility. As a result, long after the Puritans disappeared, their educational tradition survived, a legacy of their commitment to intelligence and to humane values.

Bibliographical Note

ALTHOUGH one needs patience to discover the sources of eighteenth-century educational history, luck is even more useful. For the sources are varied and scattered and sometimes hidden. Unlikely ones often yield answers to difficult questions—family papers, for example, are more helpful in reconstructing the history of curriculum than official school records. In what follows I have discussed only the most useful sources and studies.

FAMILY PAPERS, MANUSCRIPT COLLECTIONS, AND COPYBOOKS

Family papers were one of the most important sources for this study. They contain information on curriculum and textbooks, institutions, educational thought, and the lives of masters and scholars. Relatively few sets of papers covering the years before 1750 have survived; the most valuable are in the Massachusetts Historical Society. The Israel Williams Papers there contain letters about the Hadley Grammar School; and the Miscellaneous MSS, Bound and Unbound, have documents and letters which reveal much about institutions, curriculum, and educational attitudes. Even more valuable for all these matters—as well as the delightful comments on masters and scholars which they offer—are the Robert Treat Paine Papers. At the Boston Public Library the Curwin Papers have information on texts and curriculum.

For the late colonial and early national periods the following papers in the Yale University Library were useful: Baldwin Family Papers, important for curriculum, private education, and masters' lives; Park Family Papers, valuable material on Phillips Andover Academy; Thomas Mills Day Papers, especially rich on curriculum at Sharon Academy; Edwards Albert Park Collection, much material on curriculum at Phillips Andover Academy; Penniman MSS Collection, variety of material on curriculum; Silliman Family Papers, important for girls' education; Ezra Stiles Papers, scattered information on academies; Trumbull MSS Collection, useful documents on schools and academies; Jeremiah Day Papers, information on rhetoric; correspondence of Mason F. Cogswell, containing revealing letters on lives of masters and scholars; Connecticut Towns, useful material on apprenticeship and town schools.

In the Connecticut Historical Society the following are especially revealing: Daniel Goodwin Papers, rich on student life; Thomas Robbins Papers, important for curriculum; Letters to and from Ezekiel Williams, valuable on curriculum; Connecticut Towns, variety of information on schools. The nearby Connecticut State Library has the Noah Scovell Papers, which contain much on private education after the Revolution. The Letters and Papers Relating to Hopkins Academy are in the Forbes Library. The Moses Brown Papers in the Rhode Island Historical Society contain much on Providence schools. For the grammar school connected with Rhode Island College and for much else on Rhode Island education, the Brown University Miscellaneous Papers in the Brown University Library are important. The Solomon Drowne Papers, also at Brown, are valuable for study of curriculum just before the Revolution. The photostats of the William Ellery Letters in the Newport Historical Society contain important information on curriculum and late eighteenth-century attitudes toward learning.

Copybooks reveal much about curriculum and teaching. The libraries of Yale and Brown have a few, as do the Massachusetts, Connecticut, and Rhode Island Historical Societies. Others may be seen at the Forbes Library and the New Haven Colony Historical Society. But the best collection, numbering several hundred navigation, surveying, arithmetic, and mathematical copybooks, is in the Uncatalogued MSS in the Essex Institute.

DIARIES AND JOURNALS

Although I did not find many diaries and journals that contained information about education, the few I did turn up were revealing. The Benjamin Wadsworth Account Book in the Massachusetts Historical Society is a record kept by a Boston minister who became President of Harvard. Early in the eighteenth century Wadsworth boarded boys preparing in Boston schools for entrance to the College. His record of their expenses lists the names of the books he purchased for their studies. The Massachusetts Historical Society also has the Peter Burr Commonplace Book and the Ebenezer Parkman Diary. The first is the record of a Boston master and the second of a Westborough minister. Each contains much on education: Burr on students' expenses, and Parkman on the education of his own children.

The Journal of John Ballantine in the American Antiquarian Society is a valuable record kept by a Westfield, Massachusetts, minister. Ballantine prepared boys for college and his journal contains material on classical studies. In the Connecticut Historical Society Daniel Wadsworth's Diary, Amos Eaton's Journal, and an anonymous student's Diary record much on books and curriculum. The Eli Whitney Papers in the Yale University Library has Whitney's diary, kept while he was teaching school.

There are several diaries in print that reveal much about education. In *The Diary of William Bentley* (4 vols. Salem, 1905–14) there is information on post-Revolutionary curriculum; and in the *Diary of Thomas Robbins* (2 vols. Boston, 1886–87), ed. Increase N. Tarbox, there are scattered reports on teaching and exhibitions. Two records kept by girls in school are valuable: *The Diary of Julia Cowles, A Connecticut Record, 1797–1803,* ed. Laura H. Mosely (New Haven, 1931), is filled with material on the studies of girls, as is the "Diary of Charlotte Sheldon," comp. Emily Vanderpoel, in *Chronicles of a Pioneer School* (Cambridge, Massachusetts, 1903).

SCHOOL AND ACADEMY RECORDS

For the organization, finance, and management of schools and academies, I have examined a number of records. The School Committee Book, a rough manuscript account book, contains much on the Hadley Grammar School; it is in the principal's office of Hopkins Academy, the successor to the old school. The Records of Hopkins Grammar School, New Haven, in the school, contain the minutes of the trustees' meetings and much other information about finance and management of the school. The Connecticut Historical Society has the Records of the Hartford Grammar School beginning with the year 1790; the earlier records apparently have not survived. The volume which has survived contains much on curriculum and textbooks, as well as information about the finances of the school. For the grammar school in Rhode Island College see the scattered entries in Brown University Corporation Records, in Brown University Archives.

Two important sources for the study of academies are the Proprietors' Records of Plainfield Academy in the Connecticut Historical Society, and the Extracts from the Records of Phillips Academy (Andover), Park Family Papers, in the Yale University Library.

Two revealing printed sources are the "Ipswich Grammar School Documents," Colonial Society of Massachusetts, *Transactions*, 35 (Boston, 1951); and the [Minutes of] *A Meeting the 16th of January A.D. 1786* (Providence, 1786). The first contains much on the administration of the Ipswich Grammar School; the second is an elaborate description of a method of teaching arithmetic.

PUBLIC RECORDS

To reconstruct the pattern of village and city control, one must rely chiefly upon town records. They are informative on matters of finance and management of schools, and in some ways on public attitudes toward education.

Massachusetts Town Records

Because there are many Massachusetts records in print, I consulted only two in manuscript—the Woburn Town Records and the Hadley Town Records, in the Town Clerk's Office in Woburn and Hadley. Records in print: J. F. Jameson, ed., *Records of the Town of Amherst* (Amherst, 1884); *Barnstable Town Records* (Yarmouthport, Mass., 1910); *Reports of the Record Commissioners of the City of Boston* (39 vols. Boston, 1876–1909); *Records of the Town of Braintree, 1640–1793* (Randolph, Mass., 1893); *Dorchester Town Records* (Boston, 1883); *Town Records of Dudley, Mass.* (3 vols. Pawtucket, R.I., 1893–94); *Records of Duxbury* (Plymouth, 1893); *The Old Records of the Town of Fitchburg* (8 vols. Fitchburg, 1898–1913); Henry Nourse, ed., *The Early Records of Lancaster . . . 1643–1725* (Lancaster, 1884); *Records of the Town of Lee* (Lee, 1900); *Town Records of Manchester* (2 vols. Salem, 1889); *Muddy River and Brookline Records, 1634–1838* (n.p., 1875); *Records of Oxford, Mass.* (New York, 1894); *Records of the Town of Plymouth* (3 vols. Plymouth, 1889–1903); *Records of the Town of Tisbury, Mass.* (Boston, 1903); *Town Records of Topsfield, Massachusetts* (2 vols. Topsfield, 1917–20); *Watertown Records* (6 vols. Watertown, 1894–1906); *Wenham Town Records, 1730–1775* (3 vols. Salem, 1940); *Town of Weston: Records of the First Precinct, 1746–54 and of the Town, 1754–1803* (Boston, 1893); *Worcester Town Records* (6 vols. Worcester, 1879–1895).

Connecticut Town Records

The following excellent collection of manuscript town records is in the Connecticut State Library: Ashford Town Meetings, 1700–1782; Coventry Town Meetings, 1713–1782; Fairfield Town Meetings, 1661–1826; Killingly Town Meetings, 1780–1818; Norwalk Town Meetings, 1653–1707; Plainfield Town Meetings, 1699–1748; Redding Town Meetings, 1779–1847; Southington Town Meetings, 1779–1847; Wethersfield Town Votes, 1646–1716. In addition I examined with great profit the Hartford Town Votes, 1717–96, and the New London Town Meeting Records, 1740–1837, in the City Clerk's Office, Hartford and New London.

The seventeenth-century records of Hartford are in print in the Connecticut Historical Society, *Collections*, 6 (Hartford 1897). I also used F. B. Dexter, ed., *New Haven Town Records, 1649–1684* (2 vols. New Haven, 1919).

New Hampshire Town Records

I used the following MSS records on microfilm at the New Hampshire State Library: Amherst Records, Barrington Town Records, Dover Town Records, Exeter Town Records, Keene Town Records, Lebanon Town Records, Manchester Town Records, Records of Nashua, Portsmouth Town Records.

In addition several in print also proved valuable: *Early Records of Londonderry, Windham, and Derry, N.H., 1719–1762* (Manchester, N.H., 1908); *Concord Town Records, 1732–1820* (Concord, N.H., 1894); *Early Records of the Town of Derryfield Now Manchester, N.H., 1751–1782* (2 vols. Manchester, 1905).

Rhode Island Town Records

Two manuscript records were especially useful: Newport Town Meeting Records, Newport Historical Society; and Warwick Town Meeting Records, City Clerk's Office, Apponaug, R.I. And see *The Early Records of the Town of Providence* (21 vols. Providence, 1892–1915).

COURT RECORDS AND ARCHIVES

Since the courts were charged with responsibility of Massachusetts school laws, their records must be consulted. They tell much about educational performance and popular attitudes toward learning. I have used the Records of the Court of the General Sessions of the Peace for Middlesex, Essex, Worcester, Hampshire, and Berkshire Counties—in the respective offices of the clerks of the courts.

The Massachusetts Archives have much on schools, especially finance, and the gropings of the General Court in the long process of fashioning educational policy. The Connecticut Archives, in the Connecticut State Library, are less revealing, though they contain documents on both academies and schools.

STATUTES AND LEGISLATIVE RECORDS

Statutes and legislative records constitute the best sources for the study of educational policy. Most of them are well known and need not be mentioned here; they are listed in the *Harvard Guide to American History*. Two are especially valuable, for they reprint the charters of academies: *Private and Special Statutes of the Commonwealth of Massachusetts, 1780–1805* (3 vols. Boston, 1805); and Albert S. Batchellor and Henry H. Metcalf, eds., *Laws of New Hampshire* (7 vols. Bristol and Manchester, N.H., 1905–1918).

NEWSPAPERS AND MAGAZINES

Newspapers are one of the most important sources for the study of private education and for the understanding of educational thought. The most useful were the *Boston News-Letter; Boston Gazette;* [Salem] *Essex Gazette;* [Boston] *Massachusetts Centinel* (later *Columbian Centinel*); [Hartford] *Connecticut Courant;* [New Haven] *Connecticut Journal;* [New London] *Connecticut Gazette; New Haven Gazette and Connecticut Magazine* (Meigs and Dana, printers); *Newport Mercury; Providence Gazette;* [Portsmouth] *Oracle of the Day;* [Portsmouth] *New Hampshire Gazette.*

Magazines especially valuable for the essays they reprinted on educational thought: *Massachusetts Magazine; Children's Magazine; Boston Magazine; Gentleman and Lady's Town and Country Magazine; Rural Magazine, or Vermont Repository.*

USEFUL BOOKS AND ARTICLES

Although studies abound on the history of secondary education in early New England, there is very little worthy of comment in most of them. Many either praise the seventeenth-century Puritans as the founders of the public school system or denounce them for their concern with religion—which is taken to be incompatible with education. The eighteenth century is usually described as more of the same or as a period of dreary decline. Cataloguing the deficiencies in these views would be unprofitable, since it has been done in Clifford K. Shipton, "Secondary Education in the Puritan Colonies," *New England Quarterly*, 7 (1934); Samuel E. Morison, *The Puritan Pronaos* (New York, 1936, 2d ed. entitled *The Intellectual Life of Colonial New England*, 1956); and Bernard Bailyn, *Education in the Forming of American Society* (Chapel Hill, 1960). Bailyn's book itself is not without defects. I have discussed them in the *Harvard Education Review*, 31 (1961).

The educational tradition the Puritans brought with them can best be approached through a number of books: Thomas W. Baldwin, *William Shakspere's Small Latine and Lesse Greeke* (2 vols. Urbana, Ill., 1944), good on institutions and curriculum; Wallace Notestein, *The English People on the Eve of Colonization, 1603–1630* (New York, 1954), brief but especially useful for royal policy; W. K. Jordan, *Philanthropy in England, 1480–1660* (London, 1959), a revisionist account of the financing of English schools; and Samuel Eliot Morison, *The Founding of Harvard College* (Cambridge, Mass., 1935), a magisterial study of the background and founding of the first New England college. Morison's *The Intellectual Life of Colonial New England* (New York, 1956) contains a good account of seventeenth-century schools in New England, and his *Harvard College in the Seventeeth Century* (2 vols. Cambridge, 1936) is a magnificent study.

Besides Morison's *Founding of Harvard College*, two studies are helpful in understanding Puritan attitudes toward learning: Perry Miller, *The New England Mind: The Seventeenth Century* (New York, 1939); and Edmund S. Morgan, *The Puritan Family: Essays on Religion and Domestic Relations in Seventeenth-Century New England* (2d ed., Boston, 1956).

Though frequently unreliable, local histories proved helpful in establishing the number of towns that maintained grammar schools. A complete listing of them may be seen in a manuscript version of this study on deposit in the Yale University Library.

Several special studies also aided in reconstructing the village educational pattern. They are Richard Hale, *History of Roxbury Latin School* (Cambridge, 1946); Thomas B. Davis, Jr., *Chronicles of the Hopkins Grammar School, 1660–1935* (New Haven, 1938), for the school in New Haven; *History of the Hopkins Fund, Grammar School and Acad-*

emy, in Hadley Mass., 1658–1850 (Amherst, 1890); *Original Distribution of the Lands in Hartford among the Settlers,* 1639 (Coll. of Conn. Hist. Soc.); Charles W. Manwaring, *A Digest of the Early Connecticut Probate Records: Hartford District* (3 vols. Hartford, 1904–06); E. B. Greene and Virginia D. Harrington, *American Population before the Federal Census of* 1790 (New York, 1932). Oscar and Mary Handlin, *Commonwealth, A Study of the Role of Government in the American Economy: Massachusetts,* 1774–1861 (New York, 1947), offers much data which I have interpreted to explain the decline of public-supported education. Carl Bridenbaugh's *Cities in the Wilderness: The First Century of Urban Life,* 1625–1742 (New York, 1938) and *Cities in Revolt: Urban Life in America,* 1743–1776 (New York, 1956) give admirable discussions of education in Boston and Newport, though they claim too much for Newport's educational performance. Pauline Holmes, *A Tercentenary History of the Boston Public Latin School,* 1635–1935 (Cambridge, Mass., 1935), reprints a list of books used in the Latin school in 1752.

Two collections of biographies proved indispensable: Franklin B. Dexter, *Biographical Sketches of the Graduates of Yale College* (6 vols. New York, 1885–1919); and Clifford K. Shipton, *Biographical Sketches of Those Who Attended Harvard College* (11 vols. to date, Boston, 1873–1960). The first four volumes of the latter work were authored by J. L. Sibley; the last seven by Shipton, filled with learning and wit, are models of what short biography should be.

Index

Academies: appear after Revolution, 123; compete with grammar schools, 123–24; beginnings in New England, 136–37; organization, 138–53; difference between private schools and, 139; charters of incorporation, 139–40; departments, 140; government of, 140; restrictions on, 141; financing, 143–47, 150, 152; expenses of, 145; tuition, 145; curriculum, 149–50, 152, 155–58; relation to college enrollments, 150; failures, 150–51; post-Revolution pattern, 152; number of, 151–52; perpetuate liberal tradition, 152; effects on public-supported education, 153. *See also* Connecticut academies; Massachusetts academies; New Hampshire academies; Schools; *names of academies*

Academy of Plainfield, Conn., 140, 151 n.; description, 143–44; incorporation, 144; trustees recruit students, 148; exhibition at, 186

Accidence, study of, 80, 81. *See also* Cheever, Ezekiel

Adams, John, 120; quoted, 121; influenced by classics, 194

Adams, Samuel: blocks incorporation of Mass. academies, 123–24; fails to arouse support against academies, 124; influenced by classics, 194

Addington, Isaac, 55

Aesop, *Fables*, 78, 84, 154, 156

Aesthetic theory, to justify girls' education, 108

Aler, Paul, *Gradus ad Parnassum*, 86, 155

Algebra, study of, 66, 67, 92, 93, 105, 158

American Academy, New Haven, Conn., 150, 151

American Revolution. *See* Revolutionary War

Amesbury, Mass., 32

Amherst, Mass., no grammar school in, 37 n.

Amherst, N.H., has academy, 151 n.

"Ancients": definition, 120; defend classical curriculum, 120–27; defend study of Latin, 164–65

Andover Academy. *See* Phillips Andover Academy

Appropriation Act, Conn. (1793), 132; repealed (1795), 132–33

Aristotle, 88–91; on education, 189

Arithmetic, study of, 13, 16, 17, 45, 66, 71, 72, 93–96, 104, 105 n., 135, 149, 159, 167; in the colleges, 92; method of instruction, 92, 158–60; texts used for, 92–93; taught to girls, 104–05. *See also* Mathematics; *names of schools; names of textbook authors*

Ashford, Conn., hires Harvard graduate, 44

Astronomy, 64, 66, 67, 99–101, 149; method of instruction, 99–101; texts used, 100–01, 102; persistence of Ptolemaic, 101

Atkinson, James, *Epitome of the Art of Navigation*, 98 n.

Atkinson, N.H., has academy, 151 n.

Augustinian standards of reasoning, 189–90

Austin, Samuel, 176

205

BELMONT UNIVERSITY LIBRARY